Vegan
STREET
FOOD

Vegan
STREET
FOOD

FOODIE TRAVELS FROM INDIA TO INDONESIA

JACKIE KEARNEY

FOOD PHOTOGRAPHY BY CLARE WINFIELD

LONDON • NEW YORK

Senior Designer Megan Smith
Editor Kate Eddison
Production Controller Mai-Ling Collyer
Head of Production Patricia Harrington
Art Director Leslie Harrington
Editorial Director Julia Charles
Publisher Cindy Richards

Prop Stylist Tony Hutchinson
Food Stylists Jackie Kearney and
  Emily Kydd
Indexer Vanessa Bird

First published in 2015 by
Ryland Peters & Small
20–21 Jockey's Fields,
London WC1R 4BW
and
341 E 116th St
New York NY 10029
www.rylandpeters.com

Text © Jackie Kearney 2015
Design and photographs ©
Ryland Peters & Small 2015

Map illustratration (page 6)
© Lee James

ISBN: 978-1-84975-650-1

Printed and bound in China

10 9 8 7 6 5

A CIP record for this book
is available from the British
Library.

US Library of Congress
Cataloging-in-Publication Data
has been applied for.

NOTES
• Both British (Metric)
and American (Imperial plus
US cups) measurements
and ingredients are included
in these recipes for your
convenience, however it is
important to work with one
set of measurements and not
alternate between the two
within a recipe. Spellings
are primarily British.
• All spoon measurements
are level unless otherwise
specified.
• When a recipe calls for the
grated zest of citrus fruit, buy
unwaxed fruit and wash well
before using. If you can only
find treated fruit, scrub well
in warm, soapy water and
rinse before using.
• Ovens should be preheated
to the specified temperatures.
We recommend using an
oven thermometer. If using
a fan-assisted oven, adjust
temperatures according to the
manufacturer's instructions.

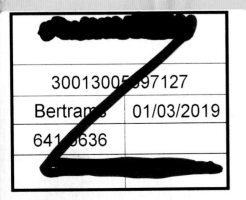

contents

INTRODUCTION
A journey into food

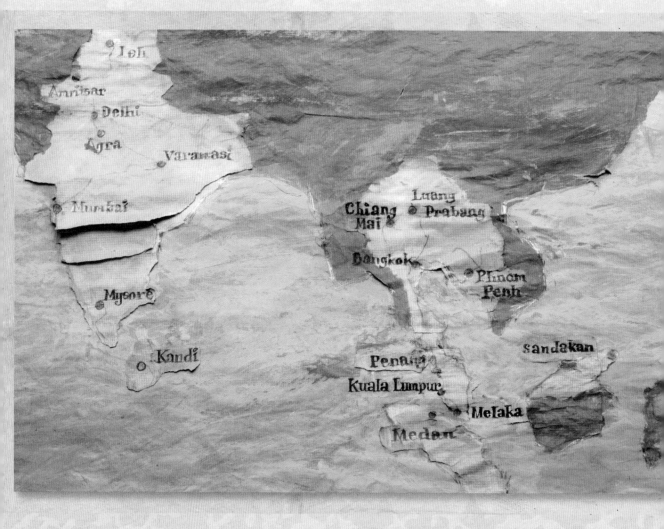

Above: A map showing some of the places the family's travels took them, hand-made by Jackie's husband, Lee.

WHEN I WAS SIXTEEN, in between wanting to be an international show jumper and a vet, I wanted to be a chef. I loved food and cooking. Most of all I loved cooking for other people. As a teenager, I was always discouraged from pursuing a career in food. In the mid-eighties, it was considered low-paid, low-status work with terrible hours. For many, it is still very much like this. But my foodie ambitions never went away. Throughout my academic career I dreamed of opening a little café, well aware that many people dream of this (like moving abroad or going travelling) and many people fail at this. Once my comfortable research career was carved out, it was even harder to change the direction. But that didn't stop me thinking about it. A lot. Some would call it an obsession.

As young children, my parents had enchanted me and my sisters with stories of their travels to faraway places during the fifties. My mum was a beautician and my dad was a hairdresser, and they took off around the world working on a cruise ship together. I used to gaze at the black and white photo of my mum posing in her bikini on a remote beach in Fiji, and wonder what it would be like to travel so far away from home. It certainly had an impact on the kind of food we grew up on, too. My mum was making curries and other considerably exotic dishes for the early seventies, although she nearly did us all in with the hottest vindaloo I've ever tasted in my life. I think I was about six, and I remember my dad had to go and brush his teeth because his mouth was on fire. Back then, who knew a glass of milk would have done the trick?

When I met Lee, we shared a mutual interest for wanting to explore the world a bit more. The idea of a 'gap year' for travel is usually seen as a choice during the heady days of singledom and youth; yet the opportunity is at a time when money and appreciation are in much shorter supply. I had always wondered about this, but especially after we had children. How can a 20 year-old possibly appreciate a year off when they have barely spent any time working or shouldering responsibilities? We fantasized about quitting our jobs and staying away until the money ran out (well actually, I was thinking about opening a little café on a Lombok hillside and not coming back at all). But then along came our twins, and we found ourselves wondering if we'd ever get there. Eventually the idea of a gap year as a family started to take shape. We worked and saved hard, and before we knew it, we had one-way tickets to Delhi and passports full of visas.

THE IDEA FOR THIS BOOK

This is a collection of recipes inspired by the food and flavours that we came across and loved during our travels. Throughout our journeys, I would jot recipes and menu ideas on the back of napkins and spend my time snacking my way around the nearest town or village. We ate together as a family for virtually every meal for an entire year. That was something new for us, too.

It's no secret how much I fell in love with Asian food, and, as a passionate cook, I was inspired to pursue my restaurant dream when we returned home. It was at that point I applied to take part in the BBC's MasterChef. I wanted to find out if my cooking was good enough to make a living from and open my own world food-inspired café. Finding the courage to travel across Asia with my family had given me the courage to try to change my working life and pursue my passion for cooking.

I love everything about the Asian culture of food. I love how accessible it is and how central it is to people's lives regardless of their background. Food, family and community come together every day, and, for us, food played a huge part of our experiences travelling as a family. I love the fresh flavours and how adaptable the food is to local and seasonal produce. And, as someone with a passion for vegan, vegetarian and sustainable food, I found that it re-ignited my love of cooking.

I have never really wanted my food to be labelled as 'vegetarian' or 'vegan'. It's a personal choice that I eat this kind of food. My passion is for food that tastes great and keeps us and our environment healthy. I want to create recipes that are adaptable to different produce and seasons, and that tell something about our journey along the way. Or maybe it's the other way round, to tell the story of our travels and something about the food along the way.

SO WHY A VEGAN BOOK?

Generally, vegan food has a poor reputation when it comes to flavour, texture and substance. There are some fantastic recipes out there, but they tend to be hidden among meat and fish ones. Or they are dishes that could be easily tweaked to be vegan, but ideas for substitutions are thin on the ground, simply don't work or are just too samey.

And this is often the source of the problem when it comes to bad vegan food: substitutions. In my experience, it's one thing to use silken tofu in pastry instead of egg yolk, but when a cook approaches vegan food only from a meat-eater's mind, they have a tendency to try to substitute the meat or fish. If I made a coq-au-vin, simply using textured vegetable protein instead of chicken, it would not taste good. There are chefs, like my food hero Yotam Ottolenghi, who transcend this. Chefs who create a plate of food that is simply about being delicious. The fact that it may be vegan or vegetarian is not the focus. This was where Asian food inspired me. Living in Manchester, I had eaten many vegan dals and curries over the years, but when we arrived in India at the start of our trip, I was absolutely blown away by what was on offer to my little vegetarian family. Not only were choices not confined to a tiny sub-section of the menu, or a substitution afterthought; they were the main act. It was now the meat or fish (and even dairy) that was confined to a sub-section. The tables had turned.

There is so much about Asian food that is more naturally vegan than Western fare, without compromising on flavour and texture. Western vegetarian food tends to centre around dairy. So much so, that my friend and I play 'halloumi bingo' when walking past the trendy restaurants in Manchester's Northern Quarter. I don't want to eat dairy as often as restaurants seem determined to feed it to me. Finding great vegan food can be a challenge when eating out, so this book aims to make sure it never happens at home.

When I started imagining this book, I thought it might be vegetarian. But once I started to write about the food from our travels that I had fallen in love with, so much of it was vegan, it seemed natural to bring that to the fore and write a collection of Asian and street food-inspired vegan recipes together in one place.

At a personal level, this has coincided with me wanting to eat more healthily, more often. Like most vegetarians, I eat too much cheese. I love creating dishes without dairy, and my fusion recipes are all about turning Asian flavours into something new and delicious. Over the last year or two, I also allowed my work-life balance to get a little out of kilter and the impact on my well-being has been notable. None of us need someone to tell us that we are what we eat. When we eat well, we start feeling (and looking) better. There's a reason veganism is so popular among the Hollywood elite. You'll live longer (and so will the planet). Over half of the planet's population lives on a vegan diet and it isn't food to be endured for health reasons. I want to celebrate vegan food in all its health-giving glory. Welcome to Vegan Street Food.

SINCE MASTERCHEF

My first year working in food (2012) was truly the mother of all crazy years! And that is really saying something given that I took part in MasterChef the year before. The food business has been the most challenging, unpredictable and rewarding thing I have ever been involved in (apart from parenthood, perhaps). It's tough. Don't let anyone ever tell you otherwise. But it's also incredibly rewarding. The joy that comes from the journey of imagining a dish to delivering that dish to an appreciative diner is a wonderful feeling. It's what brings the greatest chefs back to their restaurant kitchens every time.

At the start of 2012, I bought a 7-m/23-ft iconic Silver Bullet campervan and installed a kitchen in it. I took a commercial view of the menu and decided while it couldn't be wholly vegan or vegetarian, I would turn the usual menu structure upside-down; the menu would be at least 60 per cent vegan and vegetarian. My plan was an Asian-inspired menu with some MasterChef flair; street food-inspired dishes that were good enough for a restaurant.

I then learned how to manoeuvre a two-tonne trailer and travelled the length and breadth of the country. I got rained on, a lot. I produced some very over-ambitious menus. I was runner-up in Best Main Dish at the British Street Food Awards. I finally nailed the menus (and that elusive gross product percentage). I worked the longest hours of my life (the record being over 100 hours in a week). What do you mean there's no water access, electricity, waste disposal..?

There were some great events during 2012, some of the best ones being those you might least expect. Some of the more high-profile ones were often the hardest work with the smallest return. Smaller events that lucked out with the weather and a discerning crowd of foodies meant I got to enjoy the buzz of selling out. I drove 'Barbarella' (my kitchen on wheels) from Exeter to Edinburgh. I traded in city centres and remote villages, at food festivals, car rallies and sports events. And the feedback has been amazing, with people taking the time to tell me how much they enjoyed it.

During 2013, Barbarella had a semi-permanent location in the garden of a cask ale pub in Manchester. This gave me a chance to focus on the food rather than logistics; I immersed myself in the kitchen determined to produce restaurant-quality food with the best local produce.

I've also been running a fine-dining supperclub at my home occasionally. This has allowed me to develop new recipes, exploring the kind of fusion food I love to eat, and testing it on a discerning audience. I've included these recipes here, alongside dishes that inspired me from my travels.

A few ingredient basics

Buying Asian ingredients can be overwhelming, so here are a few essential tips. Here you will find a guide to buying spices, as well as advice on getting the best out of tofu, cooking perfect rice and making my vegan fish sauce.

THE SPICE RACK

There are many different spices and occasionally confusing variations. It's worth remembering that interchangeable names are sometimes used on packaging depending on the brand, so they have been noted alongside to help you identify them. Buying spices from mainstream supermarkets can often be expensive. I recommend a special trip to a good Indian or Asian supermarket to stock up on the core spices. Invest in some airtight containers or food bag clips to ensure your spices stay fresh. Leaving them open to the air will degrade them more than you realize. What's important to the cook is the taste, but many spices are also thought to have excellent health benefits, too.

ASAFOETIDA has a very pungent smell on its own and is used in very small quantities as a flavour-enhancer, so a little goes a long way.

BAY LEAVES are common in Indian recipes, and Indian bay leaves are slightly different with a hint of cinnamon in the flavour. I always use fresh bay leaves, as it's so easy to grow a bay tree at home.

CARDAMOM PODS can be green or black. Green pods are aromatic and floral, almost minty with a sweet edge. You can crush the pods to remove the seeds, and then pound the seeds to release all the flavour (at this point you will only need to use a very small amount). Black cardamom pods are larger and darker, with a peppery, smoky flavour.

CAROM (ajwain) has a thyme-like pungent and slightly bitter flavour, not dissimilar to cumin.

CHILLI/CHILE could have its own chapter! For the recipes here, I suggest using a good-quality chilli/chili powder, but if you can find it, buy some Kashmiri chilli/chili powder. It has a rich, deep flavour and colour, but far less heat, so it's perfect for making family-friendly dishes. Dried red chillies/chiles are easy to rehydrate and very versatile. It's also useful to have some kind of chilli/chili jam or sauce in the fridge. Either home-made (pages 33 or 101), or a store-bought sauce such as Sriracha.

CINNAMON can be powdered or whole bark. Cassia bark is very similar, with a rougher, darker-looking bark, but it is slightly sweeter with a hint of vanilla. I recommend cassia bark for Indian dishes.

CORIANDER (daniya) is available as seeds and powder. It has a warm flavour with slightly fruity citrus undertone. Always toast the seeds to release the flavour. Freshly ground powder from toasted seeds is the most delicious of all.

CUMIN (jeera) is available as seeds and powder. It is earthy and nutty, with a slightly grassy undertone. Black cumin (kala jeera) has a smokier flavour.

CURRY LEAVES release a nutty aroma and slightly citrusy flavour when fried. They are easy to find fresh in bunches from Indian or Pakistani grocers.

FENNEL SEEDS (saunf) have a warm and sweet aniseed-like flavour.

FENUGREEK has a maple-like aroma. The fresh or dried leaves are added to tomato-based dishes, and the seeds are an Indian essential.

FIVE-SPICE POWDER is a Chinese spice powder usually comprising star anise, cloves, Sichuan peppercorns, fennel seeds and cinnamon.

GARAM MASALA is a powdered Indian spice blend. It usually contains some or all of the following: black and white peppercorns, cloves, bay leaves, cinnamon or cassia bark, nutmeg (or mace), black and green cardamom pods and caraway seeds. A Punjabi mix may also contain cumin and coriander seeds, and dried ginger root.

GALANGAL (khaa in Thai) is similar to ginger but with a more peppery flavour and gentle pine aroma. The fresh root can sometimes be found in major supermarkets (usually as a paste in a jar) but more often in the fridge at a Chinese supermarket. It's useful to have some powdered at home, too.

GREEN MANGO POWDER (amchoor) brings a sour note to Indian dishes. A small packet goes a long way.

KAFFIR LIME LEAVES are found dried in major supermarkets, but I recommend buying them frozen from a Chinese grocer for a zestier aroma.

MUSTARD SEEDS are often used in tempering in Indian cooking, giving a nutty flavour to the oil. You can also buy mustard oil.

PAPRIKA is a (bell) pepper powder originating from the Iberian regions. It comes in mild and hotter versions (like spicy Spanish pimentón). Recipes here refer to the standard variety of sweet paprika.

POMEGRANATE MOLASSES is found in Indian grocery stores or even major supermarkets.

POMEGRANATE SEEDS (anardana) are dried whole seeds that bring a tangy pop of flavour to dishes.

ROOT GINGER is easy to find in most supermarkets, but a good-quality paste can be very useful.

SICHUAN PEPPERCORNS impart a slightly mouth-numbing peppery heat. One of my favourite spices.

STAR ANISE is a flower-shaped spice often used in South-east Asian dishes. You can break up the star to release the seeds and then crush them. This releases the full hit of aniseed-like flavour.

SUGAR comes in lots of forms. I avoid using palm sugar as the farming of palm products is destroying the ancient forests and jungle in South-east Asia, especially Malaysia. Alternatives include jaggery, an Indian cane sugar, or unrefined brown block sugar from Chinese supermarkets. Both have a deep caramel-like flavour. You can also use unrefined soft brown sugar.

TAMARIND has a sweet, sour and tangy flavour. You can buy wet tamarind in blocks and then soak in boiling water to make a pulp. Even if it says seedless on the packet, make sure you strain it. You can also buy tamarind concentrate/paste in jars, which has a much darker colour and stronger flavour. I prefer to use the pulp for South-east Asian recipes and I use concentrate/paste for Indian recipes. Tamarind is available in most major supermarkets, and Indian and Chinese grocers.

TURMERIC (haldi) is one of my favourite spices. I adore using the fresh root in South-east Asian recipes, but the powder makes a great substitute, and tends to work better in Indian recipes.

MAKING TOFU TASTE GOOD

I decided on this title because so many people have told me they just don't like tofu. I understand their point, as my early experiences (and some recent ones) were not good. One of the first things I didn't particularly like was the texture, and there are several ways to achieve a good texture.

FRIED TOFU PUFFS are simply deep-fried cubes or triangles of medium or firm tofu, cooked until golden brown. The oil must be hot so as not to make the tofu greasy, and the pieces drained well on paper towels. The tofu pieces can also be lightly coated in cornflour/cornstarch before frying to obtain a crispier texture. Once cooled, these puffs can be refrigerated for up to a week (or frozen). You can also buy these pre-prepared at a Chinese supermarket in the fridge section, and they are suitable for home freezing.

BAKING AND MARINATING TOFU makes for a drier and crispier nugget. Tofu puffs tend to become chewy, whereas baked tofu maintains some crispiness. After marinating (such as in ginger, five-spice or chilli/chile), it should be baked in a medium oven on a well-greased baking sheet, turning pieces occasionally to ensure even cooking. Once cooled, it can be stored in the fridge for a week (or frozen).

FREEZING TOFU changes its texture. I freeze blocks for a few days, then defrost, carefully squeezing out excess water. The tofu changes colour and texture. The layers can become fragile, so handle with care.

MAKING PERFECT RICE

For me, a rice cooker is an essential component of the Asian kitchen. They are not popular in the UK, but as soon as someone gets one, I hear them say 'I can't believe I didn't buy one earlier'.

The fact is they make perfect steamed rice every time, are quick to use and easy to clean. They last for years too, and the cheaper ones are perfectly functional and long-lasting. I suggest buying online.

Most recipes suggest the perfect balance of rice and water is 1:2. I think a little less water and some extra time for steaming is more reliable. Boil the rice in salted water until the rice is about 80% cooked. Then turn off the heat but leave on the hot stove. Stir well, add a teaspoon or two of hot water then cover the pan with a clean dishtowel and place the lid on firmly. Leave to stand for 10–15 minutes, then fluff up with a fork to ensure the rice is evenly cooked. If not, add another tablespoon of hot water, and leave to stand for 5 minutes.

VEGAN FISH SAUCE

50 g/2 oz. seaweed (such as laver, dulse or arame),
    cut into small strips
500 ml/2 cups light soy sauce or tamari
8 black peppercorns
2 garlic cloves, peeled
1 dried Chinese or shiitake mushroom

Make a batch of this vegan fish sauce and keep it in the fridge for your vegan cooking.

Add 500 ml/2 cups of water to a medium pan and add the dried seaweed. Bring to the boil and then simmer for 30–40 minutes until the water has reduced by more than half. Let stand for an hour.

Strain the mixture, reserving the liquid in another bowl. Rinse the pan and add the soy sauce or tamari, then add the peppercorns, garlic and dried mushroom. Bring to a simmer, and add the seaweed reduction. Simmer for 30–40 minutes until the mixture has reduced to less than half again. Strain and store in a sterilized glass bottle in the fridge until needed.

INDIA&
SRI LANKA

India

DELHI Nowhere smells quite like Delhi, quintessentially India to the nose. Intense in smells and activity. I had read books about lost empires, Mughal invaders and architecture, and magical djinns (spirits) that could take human and animal form. My first impressions and experiences didn't resemble my reading. Our first stay in Delhi, as for many newbie visitors, was in Pahar Ganj. An old market area close to New Delhi train station and awash with guesthouses and cheap hotels, the area attracts an array of travellers and new arrivals. Our guesthouse was as shabby and soulless as they come. And since we had arrived during the worst rainstorms that Delhi had seen for fifty years, it's fair to say Pahar Ganj wasn't looking at its best either. Delhi can be a shock for new arrivals at the best of times. And I won't lie. We were all fairly well stunned on our first stay.

On our next visit we headed to Chandni Chowk, so we could explore the oldest and busiest market in Delhi. Like most places in any Indian city, it was noisy, crowded and smelly but colourful, vibrant and exciting all at the same time. Built in the 17th century by Shah Jahan, the Mughal Emperor who built the Taj Mahal for his beloved third wife Mumtaz. The market haggling fascinated the children and the array of goods on offer was mind-blowing. We wandered amongst the lanes, drinking chai and snacking on samosas and jalebi, a rather sickly-sweet local delicacy. Needless to say the children loved it, and they were happy to find it piled high on the counter in the Indian deli back home.

It was Humayun's Tomb that finally won me over. After a torturous few days in Agra, we'd returned to Delhi with temple fatigue. The last thing I fancied was more aggressive crowds, tourists and pollution. But I let Lee talk me into visiting this architectural precursor to Agra's Taj. I'm very glad he did, as here, in this complex of tombs and garden haven, I decided there were some bits of Delhi that I really liked. I think it may have something to do with the hawkers laden with goodies, carrying trays of delicious snacks on their heads, which soon became part of our impromptu picnic.

Deep-fried fritters, pakoras and bhajis made with gram flour batter can be found all over India, and they are nearly always vegetarian, or indeed vegan. My favourites are mirchi vada. Large green chillies/chiles stuffed with dal or potato, dipped and fried in a crispy gram and turmeric batter. The children love bondas, mashed potato with coconut and green chilli/chile in batter. We first ate bondas in Sri Lanka, where they were served with pineapple, coconut and chilli/chile chutney. We had them again in the Punjab region of Northern India, usually with fiery pickles.

I make a version of these for my street food menu. I like them fairly spicy, and serve them with hot and sweet homemade pickles, hence the name, Bad Ass Bondas!

From left to right: Humayun's Tomb, Delhi; Chandni Chowk market, Delhi; Toasting peanuts, McLeod Ganj; Devotees at the Golden Temple, Amritsar; Ganges riverbank in Varanasi, Uttar Pradesh; Mysore Palace, Karnataka; Sunrise at the Golden Temple, Amritsar.

BADASS BONDAS
SPICY POTATO & SPRING ONION/SCALLION BALLS WITH COCONUT, SESAME & CHILLI/CHILE

This is my take on potato bondas, which I served in the finals for 'best snack' at the British Street Food Awards in 2012. I serve them on my menu with a trio of chutneys and pickles. You can make them a little less badass by reducing the number of chillies/chiles.

2 tablespoons desiccated/dried unsweetened shredded coconut
1 kg/2¼ lb. all-purpose potatoes, such as Maris Piper/Yukon gold
2 teaspoons garam masala
2 teaspoons sesame seeds
10 green chillies/chiles, trimmed and finely chopped
8 spring onions/scallions, thinly sliced
15-cm/6-in. piece of root ginger, peeled and finely chopped
¼ teaspoon asafoetida powder (hing)
a handful of fresh coriander/cilantro leaves, roughly chopped
1 teaspoon salt

2 tablespoons sunflower oil, plus extra for deep-frying
pickles or chutneys, to serve

BATTER
200 g/heaped 1½ cups gram flour
1 teaspoon ground turmeric
½ teaspoon chilli/chili powder
¼ teaspoon salt
a pinch of asafoetida powder (hing)
½ teaspoon baking powder

MAKES 12–18

Put the coconut in a small bowl and cover with hot water. Set aside. Put the potatoes in a pan, cover with water and boil for 15 minutes or until tender, then drain and mash. Set aside.

Toast the garam masala in a dry pan over medium heat for 30 seconds, stirring occasionally, to release the aroma, then add the sesame seeds and cook until lightly toasted, stirring occasionally. Set aside. Squeeze out the excess water from the soaked coconut.

Put all the batter ingredients in a bowl and mix together, then add 240 ml/1 cup water to make a medium-thick consistency. Heat the oil for deep-frying in a wok until hot. Test the oil with a little batter mix, to ensure that it sizzles.

Mix the potatoes with the garam masala mixture, coconut and remaining ingredients, and mould into balls the size of golf balls. Dip in the batter and gently drop into the hot oil. Fry, in batches of four or five. Cook until golden brown, turning to ensure they are evenly cooked. Drain on paper towels. Serve with a selection of your favourite pickles or chutneys.

PANI PURI POPS
CHAAT-FILLED PURI SHELLS WITH TAMARIND & POMEGRANATE

Pani puri are also known as golgappa. We first tasted them at the festival of Dussehra. Hundreds of Gods descend from the mountain villages with their statue-carrying, trumpet-blowing and drum-playing support cast – which seemed to be the entire population of the region. They arrived into the Kullu Valley and it looked like Glastonbury had come to India, with tents, food stalls and crowds everywhere. We ate many delicious snacks that day, but this dish captures the best of Indian street food – deep-fried semolina puffs (puri), stuffed with chaat (usually made with spiced potato and sprouted beans) and filled with tamarind. You can buy the puri shells, if you like, because this dish is really all about the filling.

280 g/2 cups plain/
   all-purpose flour,
   plus extra to dust
100 g/scant ⅔ cup
   semolina
a large pinch of
   bicarbonate of
   soda/baking soda
a large pinch of salt
sunflower or vegetable
   oil, for deep-frying

TAMARIND SHERBET (PANI)
1 teaspoon ground cumin
200 ml/7 oz. tamarind
   pulp, or 1 tablespoon
   tamarind concentrate/
   paste
1 teaspoon dried mango
   powder (amchoor)
½ teaspoon salt
3-cm/1-in. piece of root
   ginger
1 tablespoon fresh mint
   leaves, finely chopped
1 tablespoon fresh
   coriander/cilantro
   leaves, finely chopped

POTATO FILLING
150 g/5 oz. potatoes,
   peeled and diced into
   5-mm/¼-in. cubes
200-g/7-oz. can
   chickpeas, drained
   and rinsed
½ red onion, finely
   chopped
¼ teaspoon chilli/chili
   powder
¼ teaspoon ground
   turmeric
a pinch of chaat powder
salt, to taste

TO SERVE
Sweet Date Chutney
   (page 28)
Daniya (page 28)
2 tablespoons sev
   (fried chickpea/
   gram noodles)
natural/plain soya/soy
   yogurt
pomegranate molasses
fresh coriander/cilantro
   leaves
fresh pomegranate seeds

SERVES 8–12

Put the flour in a bowl and add the semolina, bicarbonate of soda/baking soda and salt. Add 400–600 ml/1¾–2½ cups water, a little at a time, to make a stiff dough. Knead and then leave to rest for at least 15 minutes and preferably 30 minutes.

On a flour-dusted surface, roll out the dough to about 3 mm/⅛ in. thick. Using a 4-cm/1½-in. cookie cutter, cut out about 24 small round puri discs.

Heat the oil in a wok or large, heavy pan until hot but not smoking. Gently slide 3–4 puri into the wok, using a ladle to press down gently and make them puff up. Once puffed and crisp, remove using a slotted spoon and drain on paper towels. Let cool.

To make the tamarind sherbet, toast the cumin in a dry pan over medium heat for 30 seconds, stirring occasionally, to release the aroma. Put the toasted cumin in a bowl with the other sherbet ingredients and 125 ml/½ cup water. Using a stick blender, process until smooth. Add 400 ml/1¾ cups water, and blend again. Chill for 1 hour.

Meanwhile, boil the potatoes in water to cover for 5 minutes or until tender. Drain and mix with the remaining filling ingredients. Add salt to taste.

Using a small sharp knife, crack a small hole in the centre of each puri. Fill with the potato filling, then add ¼ teaspoon each of chutney and daniya. Pour in the tamarind sherbet (a squeezy bottle is useful for this). Top with sev, and drizzle with soya/soy yogurt and pomegranate molasses. Scatter over coriander/cilantro leaves and pomegranate seeds and serve immediately.

CAULIFLOWER & KALE PAKORAS
CRISPY VEGETABLE FRITTERS

Pakoras are easy to adapt to whichever seasonal vegetables you have available. Cauliflower and kale is one of my favourite combinations, because the kale adds extra crispness. Fennel seeds and dried pomegranate seeds provide interesting pops of flavour. I always make a big batch at home, as they keep well in the fridge and can easily be reheated in the oven. Gram flour is made from chickpeas, which is a good source of protein, and has a low glycaemic index, which means the energy is released more slowly. It is also a naturally gluten-free recipe (although it's a good idea to check the asafoetida powder is gluten-free if you are serving to coeliacs/celiacs, as it can sometimes contain traces of gluten).

1 small cauliflower, cut into 2-cm/¾-in florets
1 tablespoon sunflower oil, plus extra for deep-frying
2 onions, thinly sliced
a bunch of kale or dark leaf cabbage, thinly sliced
2–4 small green chillies/chiles, to taste, finely chopped
2 large red chillies/chiles, finely chopped
1 tablespoon chilli/chili powder
½ teaspoon asafoetida powder (hing)
250 g/2 cups gram flour
2 teaspoons black cumin seeds
2 tablespoons fennel seeds
2 tablespoons dried pomegranate seeds (anardana)
a bunch of fresh coriander/cilantro, roughly chopped
¼ teaspoon bicarbonate of soda/baking soda
1 teaspoon salt
Daniya (page 28) and Raita (page 29), to serve

MAKES ABOUT 24

Parboil the cauliflower for 2–3 minutes, then drain in a colander and leave for 5 minutes.

Heat the oil in a small pan over medium heat and fry the onions for 5 minutes or until softened. Add the kale, green and red chillies/chiles, chilli/chili powder and asafoetida, and cook for 3 minutes. Set aside.

Sift the gram flour into a large bowl. Toast the cumin and fennel seeds in a dry pan over medium heat for 30 seconds, stirring occasionally, to release the aroma, then add to the gram flour followed by the onion and kale mixture. Add 120 ml/scant ½ cup water to make a thick paste, then add all the other ingredients and mix well. The batter should have a thick porridge-like consistency, so add a little more gram flour or water if necessary.

Heat the oil for deep-frying in a deep pan. Using a tablespoon, gently drop spoonfuls of the mixture into the hot oil, frying in batches of three or four. Cook until golden brown, turning halfway through to cook both sides. Remove with a slotted spoon and drain on paper towels. Serve hot, with some daniya and raita.

MIRCHI VADA
DEEP-FRIED STUFFED GREEN CHILLIES/CHILES

These fiery fritters are absolutely delicious and make a fantastic appetizer or snack. There is a large variety of chilli/chile peppers and they can vary in heat, so it's a good idea to test your batch of chillies/chiles by nibbling the end of one before using or cooking, to see how hot they are. I like to eat these fritters with raita and daniya (green chutney).

12 long, fat green chillies/chiles
sunflower oil, for deep-frying
Daniya (optional, page 28) and Raita (page 29), to serve

STUFFING
100 g/3½ oz. skinned/split mung beans or 2 potatoes, quartered
1 teaspoon cumin seeds
1 teaspoon dried mango powder (amchoor)
a handful of fresh coriander/cilantro, roughly chopped
5-cm/2-in. piece of root ginger, peeled and finely chopped

BATTER
300 g/2 heaped cups gram flour
½ teaspoon salt
¼ teaspoon ground turmeric
a pinch of baking powder

MAKES 12

Slit the chillies/chiles lengthways, about halfway down and leaving the tops intact.

For the stuffing, boil the mung beans in about 300 ml/1¼ cups water for 25–30 minutes or until they form a thick paste. Add a little more water if necessary. Alternatively, boil the potatoes in water to cover for 15 minutes or until tender, then drain and mash.

Toast the cumin seeds in a dry pan over medium heat for 30 seconds, stirring occasionally, to release the aroma. Mix all the stuffing ingredients together. Stuff the chillies/chiles with the mixture and close together – don't worry if they are not perfectly sealed as the batter will form an outer layer.

To make the batter, put the gram flour in a bowl and add the remaining ingredients. Add enough water to make a medium batter consistency (about 240 ml/1 cup).

Preheat the oven to 110°C (225°F) Gas ¼ and put a baking sheet in to warm.

Heat the oil for deep-frying in a wok or large, heavy pan. Test the oil with a little batter mix, to ensure that it sizzles. Holding it by its stem, dip a stuffed chilli/chile in the batter and carefully drop it into the hot oil. Fry on one side until the sizzling starts to ease, then turn over and cook until golden brown and crispy on all sides. Drain on paper towels and keep warm in the oven. Repeat with the remaining chillies/chiles. Serve with daniya and raita.

Clockwise from top left: Aubergine & Tamarind Chutney; Sweet Date Chutney; Cherry Tomato & Green Chilli Chutney; Daniya.

DANIYA
CORIANDER/CILANTRO (GREEN) CHUTNEY

This chutney makes an excellent condiment for any Indian food, or just with poppadums. I like to serve it with my Shashlik Skewers (page 41).

2 bunches of fresh coriander/cilantro
a bunch of fresh mint leaves
200 ml/scant 1 cup coconut milk
4–8 small green chillies/chiles, to taste, trimmed
freshly squeezed juice of ½ lemon
½ tablespoon caster/superfine sugar
¼ onion
¼ teaspoon salt

MAKES 400 ML/1¾ CUPS

Put all the ingredients in a food processor or blender and process until smooth. Taste and adjust the seasoning with salt as needed. Cover and store in the fridge for up to 1 week until needed.

SWEET DATE CHUTNEY

I use this traditional recipe in my Pani Puri Pops (page 21) and also as an accompaniment to Indian snacks such as pakoras, bhajis or poppadums.

1 teaspoon ground cumin
1 teaspoon chilli/chili powder
10 fresh Medjool dates, stoned and chopped
1 tablespoon tamarind pulp
3 tablespoons soft dark brown sugar

MAKES 250 G/9 OZ.

Toast the cumin and chilli/chili powder in a dry pan over medium heat for 30 seconds, stirring occasionally, to release the aroma.

Add the remaining ingredients with 125 ml/½ cup water. Bring to the boil and cook until the dates soften completely. Add more water if the mixture is dry, then simmer until the sauce forms a jam-like consistency. Let cool, and then store in a sterilized airtight jar in the fridge for up to 8 weeks.

CHERRY TOMATO & GREEN CHILLI CHUTNEY

This chutney is great with Badass Bondas or Mirchi Vada (pages 18 and 25), or with Indian pancakes such as Oothapam (page 64). The sweet cherry tomatoes hold a good shape and balance well with the heat from the green chillies/chiles.

1½ tablespoons sunflower oil
½ teaspoon fennel seeds
1 teaspoon mustard seeds
10 fresh or dried curry leaves
6–8 small green chillies/chiles, to taste, thinly sliced
¼ teaspoon asafoetida powder (hing)
3 tablespoons distilled or rice vinegar
½–1 teaspoon salt, or to taste
1–2 tablespoons soft dark brown sugar, to taste
1 teaspoon garam masala
500 g/3⅓ cups cherry tomatoes
a handful of fresh coriander/cilantro leaves, roughly chopped

MAKES 500 ML/2 CUPS

Heat the oil in a pan over medium heat, then add the fennel and mustard seeds and cook until they start to splutter. Add the curry leaves, then add all the remaining ingredients, except for the cherry tomatoes and coriander/cilantro leaves.

Bring to the boil, simmer gently for 4–5 minutes, then add the cherry tomatoes. Simmer until just soft, but do not simmer for too long otherwise the tomatoes will start to disintegrate. Remove from the heat, add the coriander/cilantro leaves and adjust the salt and sugar to taste. Let cool and store in the fridge for up to 2 weeks.

AUBERGINE & TAMARIND CHUTNEY

This is a very popular pickle throughout Northern India, and you see lots of versions of it on British supermarket shelves. It's not difficult to make and, since it's a proper chutney (and it keeps for months in sterilized jars), it's worth making in a large batch. I spread this on a chapati, then add shashlik vegetables (page 41) and some cachumba salad (page 48) for a delicious and filling wrap.

1 kg/2¼ lb. aubergines/
   eggplants, cut into
   thick slices
2 tablespoons salt
150 ml/scant ⅔ cup
   sunflower oil
2 onions, finely chopped
4 garlic cloves, crushed
4 large red chillies/chiles,
   finely chopped
100 g/3½ oz. piece of root
   ginger, peeled and
   finely chopped
2 teaspoons cumin seeds
2 teaspoons coriander
   seeds

1 teaspoon fenugreek
   seeds
2 tablespoons tamarind
   pulp, or 1 tablespoon
   tamarind concentrate/
   paste
1 tablespoon black
   mustard seeds
150 g/¾ cup soft light
   brown sugar
300 ml/generous 1¼ cups
   rice vinegar or cider
   vinegar

MAKES 1 LITRE/QUART

Put the aubergine/eggplant slices in a colander and sprinkle with the salt, then set aside for 1 hour. Drain off the excess liquid and wipe dry with paper towels (no need to rinse if thoroughly wiped). Place the aubergine slices in a bowl and add two-thirds of the oil. Use your hands to coat the slices in the oil.

In a frying pan/skillet, gently brown the slices well on each side until softened. Put them in a food processor or blender and pulse to make a chunky mixture – don't over-blend, as you want the aubergine to retain some texture.

Add the remaining oil to a large pan over medium heat and add the onions, garlic, chillies/chiles and ginger. Cook for 10 minutes or until soft. Meanwhile, toast the cumin, coriander and fenugreek seeds in a dry pan over medium heat for 30 seconds, stirring occasionally, to release the aroma. Finely grind the toasted spices in a spice blender or using a pestle and mortar. Dissolve the tamarind pulp or concentrate/paste in 240 ml/1 cup boiling water. Strain the juice if using pulp. Set aside.

Add the ground spices to the onion mixture with the mustard seeds, tamarind juice, sugar, vinegar and blended aubergines/eggplants. Stir well until the sugar has dissolved, then simmer gently for 30 minutes or until the mixture is thick.

Store the chutney in sterilized airtight jars, such as Kilner jars. Seal and leave for at least 1 month to mature before using. The chutney will keep for up to 12 months unopened and stored in a cool dark place. Once opened, store in the fridge and use within 1 month.

RAITA
MINT YOGURT SAUCE

This raita is traditionally made using curd or yogurt, but the flavour from the mint disguises the flavour of soya/soy yogurt, so it works as an excellent vegan substitute here.

500 g/heaped 2 cups
   natural/plain soya/soy
   yogurt
a bunch of fresh mint

leaves, finely chopped
½ teaspoon mint sauce

MAKES 500 ML/2 CUPS

Put the yogurt in a small bowl and add the mint and mint sauce. Stir well to combine. (Alternatively, you can blitz the unchopped mint with a stick blender and a few tablespoons of the yogurt, then mix this with the remaining yogurt. Don't use a blender on all the yogurt, because it breaks down the thickness of the yogurt and becomes too liquid.)

From left to right:
Taglang La, second highest
motorable pass in the world;
View of Leh, Ladakh; Young
lamas, Lamayuru.

Leh, Ladakh, Northern India

To this day, the flight into Leh is one of the most memorable journeys I have ever
experienced. Flying over the mighty Himalayan mountains is awe-inspiring of course.
The sheer size and endlessness of the landscape made us all feel very small, but it
was the moonscape of Ladakh that really took our breath away. The region has been
home to a predominantly Tibetan population since the 8th century. Buddhism and
Islam have coexisted here since the 15th century, but for me, the impact that
Buddhism came to take on my life, began here at 3500 m/11000 ft. It was also my first
introduction to Tibetan food and drink.

Not all of this was enjoyable, for my palate anyway. No matter how many times
I try it, butter tea will never be something I savour. The fatty pungent yak's butter is
just too overpowering for me. And the sweets that resemble very hard toffee, but are
in fact made of dried and hardened yak's cheese, gave my tastebuds such a surprise
I swear I nearly fainted. But the ginger tea brought me back to life and is now a firm
favourite at home. As is my favourite of all Tibetan foods, the wonderful momo.
A mouth-watering dumpling with savoury or sweet fillings, most often served with a
fiery chilli/chile dipping sauce or in a delicious broth (to which you can add the fiery
chilli/chile chutney called sepan). On a later trip, we sampled these all across Nepal
too, with the ubiquitous chilli/chile sambal, but I'm glad I first tried them in 'Little Tibet'.

TIBETAN BROTH WITH TRADITIONAL MOMOS
VEGETABLE BROTH WITH DUMPLINGS

3 carrots, roughly chopped

½ fennel bulb, roughly chopped

1 onion, roughly chopped

3 garlic cloves, roughly chopped

2 celery sticks, roughly chopped

1 main stem from a broccoli head, roughly chopped

2 tomatoes, roughly chopped

8 mushrooms, roughly chopped

2 or 3 bay leaves, to taste

a handful of fresh parsley stalks

10 black peppercorns

2 tablespoons soy sauce

1 tablespoon groundnut/ peanut oil

a handful of fresh coriander/cilantro, chopped, plus extra to serve

Tibetan Sepan, to serve (page 33)

DUMPLING WRAPPERS

200 g/1½ cups '00' flour, plus extra to dust

a pinch of salt

FILLING

2 all-purpose potatoes, such as Maris Piper/ Yukon gold

1½ teaspoons sesame oil

5-cm/2-in. piece of root ginger, peeled and finely chopped

300 g/11 oz. kale or cavalo nero, thinly sliced

1 shallot or spring onion/ scallion, finely chopped

1–2 teaspoons light soy sauce, to taste

1–2 tablespoons Shaoxing wine or dry Sherry, to taste

½ teaspoon salt

¼ teaspoon ground white pepper

SERVES 4 AS MAIN OR 6 AS AN APPETIZER

To make the dumpling wrappers, put the flour and salt in a bowl and gradually stir in a little water (about 120 ml/½ cup) to make a stiff dough. Knead well for 5–10 minutes and let rest for 30 minutes.

Put the carrots, fennel, onion, garlic, celery, broccoli stem, tomatoes and mushrooms in a large pan and cover with water. Add the bay leaves, parsley stalks, peppercorns and soy sauce. Bring to the boil and simmer gently for 40 minutes. Leave this broth to cool and then strain into a jug/pitcher. (This broth can be used immediately as a soup base or frozen for later use.)

Divide the dumpling wrapper dough into 16–18 lime-sized balls. Dust a work surface with flour. Roll out the dough thinly to about 3 mm/⅛ in. Using a 7.5-cm/3-in. cookie cutter, cut out the dumpling pastry rounds.

To make the filling, boil the potatoes in water to cover for 15 minutes or until tender, then drain and mash. Heat the sesame oil in a deep frying pan/skillet, then add the ginger and cook for a few minutes. Add the kale and cook until completely soft, then add the remaining ingredients and mix well. Set aside to cool.

Return the broth to the pan and reheat for serving. Using a pastry brush, moisten the outside edge of a pastry round with water. Add a teaspoonful of the filling to the centre and, holding it in the palm of one hand, use the other hand to fold it over to form a half-moon shape, and then crimp the edges by making little folds with your thumb. (Alternatively, the dumplings can be folded like little money-bags. Holding the wrapper with filling in the palm of one hand, bring all the edges together then twist the top to seal.) Repeat with the remaining wrappers. The dumplings should be cooked the same day or they can be frozen and cooked from frozen.

Put a large pan over high heat and add the groundnut/peanut oil. Put the dumplings in the hot pan and cook until the underneath starts to turn golden brown. Add 145 ml/generous ½ cup cold water, and quickly cover with a lid. Steam the dumplings for 7–10 minutes (depending on the size of dumpling and the thickness of pastry) until they are translucent.

Ladle the hot broth into bowls and add three or four dumplings to each. Scatter a little fresh coriander/cilantro on the top. Serve with Tibetan sepan, which can be added to the soup at the table to taste.

TIBETAN SEPAN
CHILLI/CHILE CHUTNEY

This traditional recipe is a fresh chutney and will therefore keep for only about a week in the fridge. You can use it like a pistou for adding to a soup broth or simply serve it as a dip for momos (page 32) or pakoras (page 22).

2 tablespoons vegetable oil
3–4 garlic cloves, to taste, roughly chopped
1 red onion, thickly sliced
2 celery sticks, thickly sliced
2 large red chillies/chiles, thickly sliced
2 tomatoes, quartered

3–4 spring onions/scallions, thickly sliced
a handful of fresh coriander/cilantro leaves, roughly chopped
salt, to taste

MAKES 450 ML/SCANT 2 CUPS

Heat the oil in a large frying pan/skillet and add the garlic and red onion. Cook gently for 5–10 minutes until softened.

Add the celery, chillies/chiles and tomatoes, and cook for a further 5 minutes or until the tomatoes start to soften. Add the spring onions/scallions and fresh coriander/cilantro and cook gently for a further 1–2 minutes until the spring onions/scallions are softened.

Using a food processor or blender, gently blitz the mixture. Do not overblend; it should be a little chunky, not smooth. Season to taste with salt and set aside to cool.

SIMPLE SAMBAL
SPICY CHILLI/CHILE & GARLIC SAUCE

Sambal is found all across Asia (and beyond), and this version is my favourite simple recipe. It can be served with all manner of snacks and dishes. Roasting the chillies/chiles and garlic gives it a deep, smoky flavour, and you can add more maple syrup or sugar if you want to make it less spicy.

500 g/1 lb. 2 oz. large red chillies/chiles, trimmed
1 garlic bulb, separated in cloves, unpeeled
2 tablespoons light soy sauce, or tamari if making gluten-free
1 tablespoon Shaoxing wine or dry Sherry (optional)
2 tablespoons maple

syrup, or to taste
2 tablespoons soft dark brown sugar, or to taste
1 teaspoon salt, or to taste
125 ml/½ cup sunflower or vegetable oil

2 baking sheets, greased

MAKES 400 ML/1½ CUPS

Preheat the oven to 220°C (425°F) Gas 7.

Lay the chillies/chiles on one baking sheet and the garlic cloves on another. Bake the chillies for 10–15 minutes until they are well roasted and starting to blacken at the edges. Bake the garlic for 8–10 minutes until golden brown and sticky.

Peel the garlic cloves and then put all the ingredients in a food processor or blender and blend to make a smooth paste. Adjust the seasoning of maple syrup, sugar and salt to taste. This is a very spicy sauce, but it should have a sweet edge. Store in an airtight container in the fridge for up to 4 weeks.

WILD MUSHROOM & NASTURTIUM MOMOS
SEASONAL DUMPLINGS

This is a foraging-based recipe for momos, which illustrates the different fillings that can be used. I created these for a pop-up dining event during the autumn/fall and wanted to use local produce. My garden was overrun with nasturtiums at the time, and the leaves were the size of large plates. My MasterChef buddy Tim Anderson thought we should make tamales with them, such was their size. Their peppery iron-rich flavour makes a good substitute for dark cabbage, which can often be used in the filling.

200 g/1½ cups '00' flour, plus extra to dust
a pinch of salt
1 tablespoon groundnut/peanut or vegetable oil
Simple Sambal (page 33), to serve

FILLING
1½ teaspoons sesame oil
1 onion, finely chopped
5-cm/2-in. piece of root ginger, peeled and finely chopped
2 garlic cloves, finely chopped
200 g/7 oz. wild mushrooms or chestnut and/or oyster mushrooms, chopped
150 g/5 oz. firm tofu, crumbled
1 tablespoon finely chopped fresh coriander/cilantro
200 g/7 oz. nasturtium leaves, thinly sliced
1–2 teaspoons light soy sauce, to taste
½ teaspoon salt
2 pinches of ground white pepper

MAKES 15–20

Put the flour and salt in a bowl and gradually stir in a little water (about 120 ml/½ cup) to make a stiff dough. Knead well for 5–10 minutes and leave to rest for 30 minutes.

To make the filling, add the sesame oil to a deep frying pan/skillet over medium heat, then add the onion, ginger and garlic, and cook for 5 minutes. Add the mushrooms to the pan, and cook for 5 minutes more. Add the remaining ingredients and mix well. The nasturtium leaves will wilt immediately, and do not need further cooking. Set aside to cool.

Dust a work surface with flour. Roll out the dough thinly to about 3 mm/⅛ in. thick. Using a 7.5-cm/3-in. cookie cutter, cut out small round discs.

Using a pastry brush, moisten the outside edge of the pastry round with water. Add a teaspoonful of the filling to the centre and, holding the pastry in the palm of one hand, use the other hand to fold it over to form a half-moon shape, and then crimp the edges by making little folds with your thumb. Repeat with the remaining pastry rounds (wrappers).

Heat the groundnut/peanut oil in a pan over high heat. Put the dumplings in the hot pan and cook until the underneath starts to turn golden brown. Add 145 ml/generous ½ cup cold water, and quickly cover with a lid. Steam the dumplings for about 7–10 minutes (depending on the size of dumpling and the thickness of pastry) until they are translucent. Serve with simple sambal.

PEMA'S PIZZA MOUNTAIN
VEGETABLE CHAPATI PIZZA

The trek from Leh to Lamayuru took us almost five days. We had a Tibetan guide called Pema, who lived in a refugee camp just north of Leh. He loved food, and we had lengthy discussions about traditional dishes as well as his Western favourites. One evening, we had access to a wood-fired oven and he made chapati pizzas. The children called it 'Pema's pizza mountain', as it was piled so high with vegetable toppings.

220 g/1⅔ cups chapati
  flour
½ teaspoon salt
½ teaspoon ajowan
  (carom) seeds
vegetable oil, for greasing
2 tablespoons grated
  vegan Parmesan
  (optional)
1 large chilli/chile,
  trimmed and thinly
  sliced (optional)
fresh coriander/cilantro
  sprigs, to garnish

TOMATO SAUCE

1 tablespoon vegetable
  or sunflower oil
1 onion, thinly sliced
2 garlic cloves, crushed
1 teaspoon paprika
salt and ground white
  pepper
8 tomatoes, chopped

TOPPINGS

1 tablespoon vegetable
  or sunflower oil
20 chestnut or button
  mushrooms, sliced
1 red (bell) pepper,
  deseeded and sliced
  into thin strips
1 yellow (bell) pepper,
  deseeded and sliced
  into thin strips
1 green (bell) pepper,
  deseeded and sliced
  into thin strips
1 courgette/zucchini,
  thinly sliced
2–3 large handfuls of
  baby spinach leaves

*large pizza stone or
baking sheet*

MAKES 4

Sift the flour with the salt into a bowl and stir in the ajowan seeds. Stir in about 150 ml/⅔ cup water until the mixture forms a soft, pliable dough, then knead well for 10 minutes. Cover with a damp dish towel and leave to rest for 30 minutes.

To make the sauce, heat the oil in a small pan over medium heat and cook the onion for 5 minutes or until soft. Add the garlic, paprika and a little salt and white pepper. Cook for a further 2 minutes, and then add the chopped tomatoes. Simmer gently for 10–15 minutes until soft and well reduced. Let cool.

Preheat the oven to 220°C (425°F) Gas 7. Place a pizza stone or baking sheet in the oven to heat up.

For the toppings, heat the oil in a large frying pan/skillet over high heat. Add all the vegetables, except the spinach, and cook for 3–4 minutes until they start to soften and brown a little.

Divide the dough into four balls, then lightly oil your hands and a dough ball. Roll one ball out to 3 mm/⅛ in. thick. Brush some oil onto the hot pizza stone or baking sheet and carefully put the dough onto it, then brush the top with a little oil. Bake for 6–8 minutes until almost cooked.

Spread the tomato sauce over the base, about 3 mm/⅛ in. thick. Layer the spinach and then the cooked vegetables on top like a pizza, ensuring the thickness of the vegetables is double that of the base. Put a few small dollops of the tomato sauce in between the vegetables, add a drizzle of oil and a pinch of salt and white pepper. Bake for 8 minutes until the vegetables are cooked and the base is browned around the edges. Scatter with vegan Parmesan and chilli/chile, if you like. Repeat to make four pizzas in total.

From left to right: Road trip from Ladakh, Jammu and Kashmir; Local house, Old Manali; Manali view, Himachel Pradesh.

Into Manali, Himachel Pradesh, Northern India

I read about the road trip between Leh and Manali before we left the UK. It's a famous route and journeys through the surreal moonscape of Ladakh into the mountainous green and rather Alpine-looking Himachel Pradesh. My favourite lunch stop was at the Gorges of Pang, where we ate dal and chapatis at a roadside tent, part of an encampment for the Himank Road Builders. Mostly Tibetan refugees, these workers toil in tar and stone while they attempt to keep the roads open on an ever-shifting landscape for extremely low wages. The workers waved and cheered at the children as we passed. The gorges themselves surrounded us like some kind of mini Grand Canyon sculpted from sand. Bizarre and beautiful at the same time.

It took three full days of driving to reach Manali, and our spines felt battered and compressed. Manali is divided into the old and new town, so we stayed in a lovely guesthouse halfway in-between. The area felt quite touristy after the peaceful space of Leh, but we were spoilt for choice with good places to eat. For me, the highlight was definitely Mama's Café. She taught me how to make the stuffed parathas we all loved, and she made veggie burgers for the children, so they could have a little taste of home. Manali was also where Roisin decided her favourite dish was makhani dal, and proceeded to order it wherever we went.

MAMA-JI'S STUFFED PARATHAS
FLATBREADS STUFFED WITH CAULIFLOWER & POTATO

Mama's Café is in new Manali town. We often ate here for breakfast, enjoying the aloo-stuffed parathas with a fresh bowl of curd. Mama also made some excellent spicy veggie burgers, which reminded the children of home, so they loved it there. Our relationship with the family who run the café became much closer after Mama's husband, a retired Delhi doctor, took care of me when I was very ill. Lee and the children had been in the café without me and he was concerned. So each day, Lee returned with a special package for me. Sometimes it was simple food like rice or a boiled egg, sometimes medicines or herbal supplements. After a week, I was well enough to make the trip into town from our hillside retreat. Mama made me my favourite stuffed paratha and curd. The day we left Manali, they presented us with a book about drawing journeys, instead of taking photographs. It was quite an emotional departure for us all. In India, when you respect or love someone, you add 'ji' to the end of their name or title. I will never forget the kindness this family bestowed on my family. Mama-Ji taught me her paratha recipe before I left.

500 g/3¾ cups fine chapati flour or '00' flour, plus extra to dust
1 teaspoon salt
1 teaspoon ajowan (carom) seeds
vegetable oil, for frying
The Hungry Gecko's Dal Masala (page 45) or Raita (page 29), to serve

FILLING
3 small all-purpose potatoes, such as Maris Piper/Yukon gold
2 large red chillies/chiles, finely chopped
1 small green chilli/chile, finely chopped
½ teaspoon dried mango powder (amchoor)
¼ cauliflower, grated
a small handful of fresh coriander/cilantro leaves, chopped

MAKES 4–6

Sift the flour and salt into a bowl and stir in the ajowan seeds. Stir in about 110 ml/scant ½ cup water until the mixture forms a soft, pliable dough and knead well for 10 minutes. Cover with a damp dish towel and leave to rest for 30 minutes.

To make the filling, boil the potatoes in water to cover for 15 minutes or until tender, then drain and mash. Add the chillies/chiles to the potato with the mango powder and grated cauliflower. Season with salt and stir in the coriander/cilantro.

Roll the dough into even-sized balls, about 5 cm/2 in. diameter. Dust a work surface with flour. Roll out 1 ball evenly into a large circle approximately 3 mm/⅛ in thick. Spoon some filling into the centre of the dough and spread it out thinly to cover the centre of the dough, leaving a good 5-cm/2-in. border.

Fold the dough into the centre, making 6–8 folds around the entire paratha and bringing the outer edge to the centre (like bringing up the sides of a parcel). Gently roll the paratha again, taking care not to apply too much pressure, and carefully pushing any air out of the centre. Roll gently until you have a 12–15-cm/4½–6-in. disc, about 5 mm/¼ in. thick. Repeat with the remaining dough balls and filling.

Gently heat 1 tablespoon of vegetable or sunflower oil in a large frying pan/skillet. Fry a paratha until golden on both sides. Drain on paper towels to remove the excess oil. Repeat with the remaining parathas. Using a pizza slicer, cut each paratha into 4–6 large triangles or serve whole. Serve with dal masala or simply some raita.

SHASHLIK SKEWERS
SHASHLIK MARINATED VEGETABLES

I made this dish for my MasterChef audition. I worked on this recipe for months, tweaking and adjusting it and trying to perfect it. The paste is incredibly packed with flavour, and is extremely versatile. It can even be used as a base for a curry. We ate shashlik paneer and vegetables in many places in India, from a café in McLeod Ganj to Goa's supposedly finest tandoor in Panjim, the Sher-E-Punjab. I based this recipe on my favourite version served at The Green Hotel in Mysore, where we stayed for a birthday treat. The Chittaranjan Palace, the former home to the Raj's sisters, has been restored into a model of sustainable tourism by the Charities Advisory Trust, where all profits are distributed to charitable and environmental projects in India. As well as making the best shashlik I've ever tasted, they also have heart-warming policies of employing widows and other excluded women on the staff. It is a truly wonderful place to stay, right down to the mosquito-eating fish in the pond! The Black Chickpea Pilaf (page 42) accompaniment is based on some techniques I learned from my Gujarati friend Hajit.

1 green (bell) pepper, deseeded and cut into 2.5-cm/1-in. pieces

1 red (bell) pepper, deseeded and cut into 2.5-cm/1-in. pieces

1 onion, cut into 2.5-cm/1-in. pieces

8–10 chestnut mushrooms

1 courgette/zucchini, cut into thick slices

SHASHLIK MARINADE
2 large red chillies/chiles, trimmed

4 green bird's-eye chillies/chiles, trimmed

6 garlic cloves, peeled and left whole

5-cm/2-in. piece of root ginger, peeled

2 tablespoons vegetable oil

2 teaspoons ground cumin

1 teaspoon ground coriander

1 teaspoon garam masala

½ teaspoon ground turmeric

2 teaspoons ground paprika

½ teaspoon chilli/chili powder

2 tablespoons freshly chopped coriander/cilantro leaves

2 tablespoons tamarind concentrate/paste

1 tablespoon soft brown sugar

2 tablespoons cornflour/cornstarch

4 tablespoons white wine vinegar

2–3 tablespoons plain soya/soy yogurt, or to taste

salt and freshly ground black pepper

Black Chickpea Pilaf (page 42), to serve or warmed chapati wrap, if preferred

Daniya (page 28) or Cachumba Salad (page 48) and Aubergine & Tamarind Chutney (page 29), to serve

8 bamboo skewers, soaked in cold water

SERVES 4

Preheat the oven to 220°C (425°F) Gas 7.

To make the shashlik marinade, put the chillies/chiles, garlic and ginger in a roasting pan and drizzle with the vegetable oil. Toss to combine. Roast for 8–10 minutes or until well browned. Remove from the oven and cool slightly.

Toast the ground spices in a dry frying pan/skillet over high heat for 2 minutes, stirring occasionally, to release the aroma. Put in a small food processor with the roasted chillies, garlic and ginger, add the fresh coriander/cilantro, tamarind concentrate/paste, sugar, cornflour/cornstarch and vinegar, and blend until smooth. Season with salt and pepper. The paste will keep in the fridge for up to a month.

Put 4 tablespoons of the marinade in a bowl and stir in the yogurt (you can make it less spicy by adding more yogurt, if you like). Add the vegetables, tossing to make sure all the pieces are well coated. Cover the bowl with clingfilm/plastic wrap and chill in the fridge for at least 20 minutes.

Preheat the grill/broiler to high. Thread the vegetables onto the soaked skewers, covering any exposed bamboo with foil to prevent it from burning. Grill/broil the vegetable skewers for 5–6 minutes on each side until golden brown.

Serve the shashlik skewers on the black chickpea pilaf with a ramekin of daniya. The shashlik vegetables are also delicious served in a warmed chapati wrap with cachumba salad and aubergine and tamarind chutney.

BLACK CHICKPEA PILAF

1 tablespoon vegetable oil
½ onion, thinly sliced
1 garlic clove, crushed
5-cm/2-in. piece root ginger, peeled and thinly sliced
10 black peppercorns
4 pieces cassia bark/cinnamon
7 cloves
8 green cardamom pods
2 black cardamom pods

½ teaspoon salt
ground white pepper
200 g/generous 1 cup basmati rice, rinsed
200 g/7 oz. canned brown chickpeas (kala channa), drained and rinsed
100 g/1¼ cups flaked/slivered almonds

SERVES 4

Heat the oil in a large pan over medium-low heat, add the onion and fry very gently for 15–20 minutes until softened, caramelized and light brown. Add the garlic, ginger, peppercorns, cassia bark/cinnamon, cloves, cardamom pods, and salt and pepper, and fry for 2–3 minutes. Add the rice, and fry for 2 minutes, stirring occasionally. Add the chickpeas and 250 ml/generous 1 cup water. Cook over medium–high heat for 7–8 minutes until the rice is 80 per cent cooked, adding a little extra water if the rice starts to dry out. Remove the rice from the heat, cover with a clean dish towel and put a lid on top. Leave to stand for 10 minutes.

Meanwhile, toast the almonds in a dry frying pan/skillet over medium heat for 30 seconds, until golden brown, then leave to cool.

Fluff up the rice with a fork and stir the toasted almonds through before serving.

THE HUNGRY GECKO'S DAL MASALA
YELLOW DAL WITH AUBERGINE/EGGPLANT MASALA

This dish was inspired by our roadside stops as we travelled across India. Every darbar has its own version of yellow dal, served with freshly made flatbreads. The art of dal is in the tempering, which provides the key flavours cooked in oil or butter that is then poured over the cooked pulses before serving. I made a version of this dish during a MasterChef invention test, and served it with a cauliflower-stuffed paratha. It's since become a big seller on my street-food menu, especially during the colder months, as it's warming and filling. Indian comfort food, pure and simple!

100 g/generous ½ cup red lentils

100 g/½ cup split and skinned mung dal

100 g/½ cup split non-oily toor dal

4 bay leaves

1 teaspoon ground turmeric

2 garlic cloves, peeled and left whole

2 whole large red dried chillies/chiles, trimmed

1 teaspoon salt

a handful of fresh coriander/cilantro leaves, roughly chopped

lemon wedges, soft chapatis or Mama-Ji's Stuffed Parathas (page 40), to serve

AUBERGINE/EGGPLANT CURRY (BRINJAL BHAJEE)

2 large aubergines/ eggplants, cut into 4-cm/1½-in. cubes

1 large onion, cut into 2.5-cm/1-in. pieces

1 green (bell) pepper, deseeded and cut into 2.5-cm/1-in. pieces

350 ml/1½ cups vegetable oil

4 teaspoons garam masala

1 teaspoon chilli/chili powder

1 large red chilli/chile, trimmed and thinly sliced

2 teaspoons salt

a pinch of sugar

TEMPERING FOR THE DAL

2 tablespoons vegetable oil

10 garlic cloves, thinly sliced

8 fresh or dried curry leaves

½ teaspoon black mustard seeds

a squeeze of lemon juice

salt, to taste

SERVES 4–6

Put the red lentils and dal in a large, heavy pan. Add the bay leaves, turmeric, garlic, whole dried chillies/chiles, salt and 570ml/2½ cups cold water. Bring to the boil, then skim off the foam. Simmer gently for 45 minutes or until the lentils have broken down and the mung beans are soft. Add more water if needed, so that it has the consistency of a medium-thick soup.

To make the aubergine/eggplant curry, put the aubergines/eggplants, onion and green (bell) pepper in a large pan over medium heat and add the 350 ml/1½ cups vegetable oil, the spices, salt and sugar. Cover the pan and cook for 15–20 minutes, stirring frequently, or until the aubergine/ eggplant is completely soft. Drain off the excess oil before serving (you can keep this in the fridge to use as a curried oil for frying, if you like).

To make the tempering, heat the 2 tablespoons of oil in a small frying pan/skillet over medium heat, add the garlic and cook for 3 minutes or until starting to brown. Add the curry leaves and mustard seeds, and cook until the seeds start popping.

Pour the tempering over the cooked dal. Stir well and add the lemon juice and salt. Adjust the seasoning if necessary. To serve, pour the yellow dal into a pasta bowl and place a spoonful of the aubergine/eggplant curry in the centre. Sprinkle with fresh coriander/cilantro and serve with a wedge of lemon, chapatis or stuffed parathas.

ROISIN'S EASY MAKHANI DAL

CREAMY BLACK DAL WITH TOMATO

There are plenty of complicated recipes for makhani dal out there, but as this is my daughter's favourite comfort food, I had to develop a recipe that was easier and quicker to make at home. The whole urad dal and dried kidney beans require soaking overnight, but for a quicker version you can use split urad dal and soak it for just 1–2 hours and use canned red kidney beans. I think the tomato purée/paste adds a creamy consistency as well as being quicker than fresh tomatoes, which would be more traditional. I use almond cream because I like the taste, but you can also use soya/soy cream instead.

220 g/generous 1 cup whole black urad dal, soaked overnight and drained, or use split dal and soak for 1–2 hours, if short of time

80 g/generous ½ cup dried red kidney beans, soaked overnight and drained, or 400 g/14 oz. canned kidney beans, rinsed and drained

5-cm/2-in. piece of root ginger, grated

2 small green chillies/chiles

6 garlic cloves, crushed

4 tablespoons vegetable oil

2 small or 1 large onion, finely chopped

3 tablespoons tomato purée/paste, or 4 large tomatoes, chopped

2 tablespoons ground coriander

1 teaspoon ground cumin

¼ teaspoon Kashmiri chilli/chili powder, or ¼ teaspoon paprika and a pinch of chilli/chili powder

½ teaspoon asafoetida powder (hing)

1 tablespoon garam masala

4 tablespoons almond or soya/soy cream

a large handful of fresh coriander/cilantro leaves

salt and ground white pepper

SERVES 4–6

Put the soaked dal and soaked kidney beans in a large pan and add the ginger, chillies/chiles, garlic and 1.2 litres/5 cups water. Bring to the boil and simmer for 50 minutes or until tender. If using canned beans, cook the dal for 45 minutes, and then add the beans and bring back to a simmer for 10 minutes. Add more water if it gets too thick. Season with salt and white pepper.

Heat 2 tablespoons of the oil in a pan over medium heat and fry the onions for about 10–15 minutes until golden brown, then add the tomato purée/paste and 500 ml/generous 2 cups water (or 150 ml/½ cup if you are using fresh tomatoes). Add the coriander, cumin and chilli/chili powder. Simmer for 10 minutes. Add the tomato mixture to the dal and beans, and bring to a simmer for another 15 minutes until well cooked.

Heat the remaining 2 tablespoons of vegetable oil in a small frying pan/skillet over medium heat and add the asafoetida and garam masala. Stir for 1 minute, then pour this over the dal. Stir into the mixture and remove the pan from the heat. Add a swirl of almond cream and garnish with coriander/cilantro to serve.

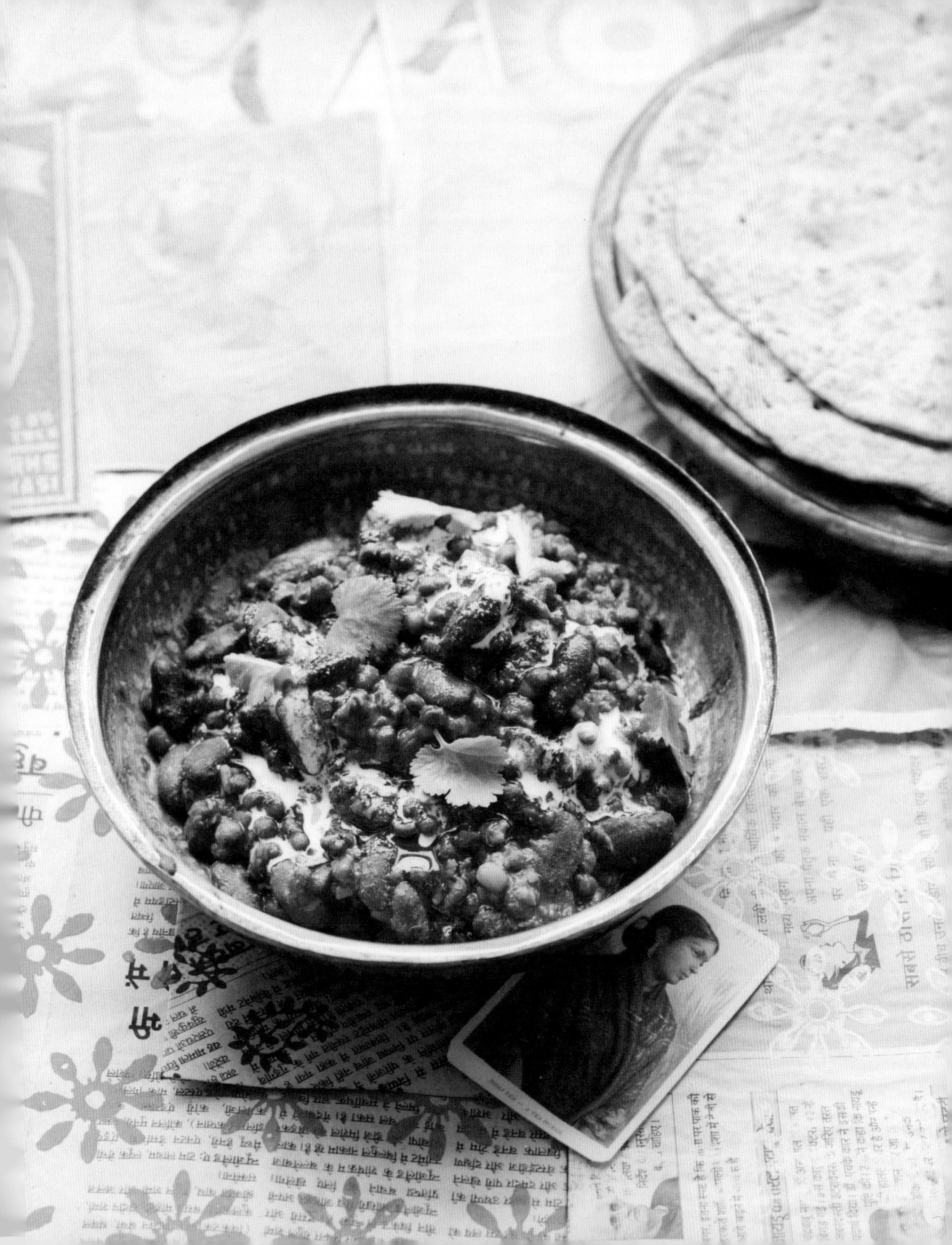

Amritsar to Varanasi

The city of Amritsar sits close to the Pakistan border, and drew us in immediately. We explored the city on the back of cycle rickshaws, as the same drivers waited outside our guesthouse every day promising to take us to some new delight, often involving food. The Punjab 'bread basket' region sits across the north-west of India and north-east Pakistan, and with its plentiful produce, is home to some of the best food in the country.

Groups of Sikh school children waved excitedly to us from the back of their rickshaw and we were welcomed at The Golden Temple like long lost family. We were so overwhelmed with the huge temple complex and the people there, we returned at sunrise the following day to experience some more Sikh hospitality. The temple feeds over ten thousand people every day, and anyone is welcome to come and eat. People from all walks of life and from across the city participate in helping, with groups of people sitting on the floor making thousands of chapatis, alongside huge vats of dal and giant tandoor ovens. We pitched in with the washing up after enjoying our simple but delicious meal of dal, rice and chapati.

Top left: Pathankot school children, Punjab.

CACHUMBA SALAD
CHOPPED SALAD WITH FRESH HERBS & LEMON

Cachumba (or kachumba) is simply the name in India for a chopped salad, usually mixed with some fresh herbs and lemon juice. It also happens to be the name of one of my favourite Manchester restaurants. This salad is the perfect accompaniment to any Indian dish, and keeps for a day or two in the fridge.

1 cucumber, halved
  lengthways
3 tomatoes, halved, cored
  and cut into 1-cm/½-in.
  pieces
1 red onion, cut into
  1-cm/½-in. pieces
a handful of fresh mint
  leaves, chopped

a handful of fresh
  coriander/cilantro
  leaves, chopped
freshly squeezed juice
  of 1 lemon

SERVES 4–6

Using a teaspoon, scrape out the watery seeds from the centre of the cucumber. Slice the flesh into 1-cm/½-in. lengths, and then into dice. Put the cucumber in a serving bowl.

Add the remaining ingredients and mix well. Do not add salt before serving or the salad will become watery.

KOFTA MASALA
GOURD & CASHEW KOFTAS IN AUBERGINE/EGGPLANT MASALA

This dish has many names depending on what the koftas are made from. When it comes to my street food trailer, the name will also depend on where they are being served – the festival trend is for cool puns these days (these appear as 'Dude, Where's My Kofta' on my festival menus). I've tried grating lots of different vegetables into these kofta balls, but I do enjoy doodhi. It's a type of Indian gourd, which comes in various shapes and sizes, and is available in many Indian grocers. I use the bottle gourd, which looks like a light-green elongated squash.

120 g/1 cup cashew nuts
2 bottle/doodhi gourds, peeled and grated
375 g/3 cups gram flour
2 large red chillies/chiles
1 teaspoon ginger paste
1 teaspoon garlic paste
a large handful of fresh coriander/cilantro
1 teaspoon chaat masala
1 teaspoon salt, or to taste
vegetable oil, for shallow-frying
steamed basmati rice, Cachumba Salad (page 48) and Raita (page 29), to serve

MASALA SAUCE
2 aubergines/eggplants, roughly chopped
1 teaspoon salt, or to taste
2 tablespoons vegetable oil, plus extra to grease
2 onions, thinly sliced
1 tablespoon ginger paste
1 tablespoon garlic paste
½ teaspoon ground turmeric

1 teaspoon ground cumin
2 teaspoons ground coriander
1 teaspoon Kashmiri chilli/chili powder, or ½ teaspoon chilli/chili powder and ½ teaspoon paprika
4 small green chillies/chiles, finely chopped
2 x 400-g/14-oz. cans chopped tomatoes
1 teaspoon garam masala
1 heaped tablespoon dried methi/fenugreek leaves, or ½ bunch of fresh leaves, roughly chopped

baking sheet, greased

SERVES 4–6

Toast the cashew nuts in a dry pan/skillet over medium heat for 1–2 minutes, stirring occasionally, until golden. Put the grated gourds in a colander and drain the excess liquid, squeezing the grated flesh to remove as much water as possible. Put the flour in a bowl and add the chillies/chiles, cashews, ginger and garlic pastes, fresh coriander/cilantro, chaat masala and salt. Add 240–360 ml/1–1½ cups of water to form a thick paste. Taste the paste and add more salt if necessary.

Half-fill a frying pan/skillet with oil and place over medium heat. Wet your hands and form the mixture into 16–18 loose balls each about the size of a golf ball. Gently drop the koftas into the oil and fry in batches until golden brown and cooked through (do not overcrowd the pan). Drain on paper towels.

Preheat the oven to 220°C (425°F) Gas 7.

To make the masala sauce, put the aubergines/eggplants on the prepared baking sheet and sprinkle over the salt. Roast for 20–30 minutes until browned. Heat the oil in a large pan over medium heat and cook the onions for 5 minutes or until softened. Add the ginger, garlic, spices and fresh chillies/chiles, then fry for 3 minutes more. Add the tomatoes and garam masala. Bring to the boil, then simmer gently for 10–15 minutes until thickened. Add the aubergines/eggplants and simmer for 10 minutes or until the mixture is thick. Using a stick blender, blend until smooth. Add the methi/fenugreek and stir well. Season with more salt if necessary. Add the koftas and simmer gently, being careful not to break the koftas.

Clockwise from top left:
The Hungry Gecko's Dal Masala;
Simple Sambal; Sunil's Dal;
Baigan Ka Bharta.

BAIGAN KA BHARTA
AUBERGINE/EGGPLANT MASH

We ate a number of delicious vegetable mash dishes along our journey. I have fond memories of eating pav bhaji along Chowpatty beach in Mumbai (bhaji simply means vegetable in Maharashtrian). One of Mumbai's ultimate street food snacks, a richly spiced vegetable mash (bhaji) is served alongside a soft roll (pav or pao is the Portuguese word for small bread). So you could substitute the aubergine/eggplant for mashed potato and peas, to make a delicious alternative. Personally I adore the texture of the aubergines/eggplants in this Punjabi-inspired recipe, which I often eat with bread as it just begs to be scooped onto your chapati or paratha.

The dish also makes a great element on a thali platter (an Indian selection plate of several dishes) alongside some shashlik and dal. You could put the aubergines/eggplants onto a barbecue/outdoor grill to blacken and recreate the smoky taste (as this is usually done in a tandoor), but a hot oven or grill/broiler works equally well. I sometimes make this recipe using fresh turmeric root, and roast pieces inside the aubergine/eggplant along with the garlic cloves. But it's not an ingredient that's easy to come by, but if you do see it, you should definitely try it.

4 large aubergines/
  eggplants
8 garlic cloves
4 cloves
3–5 tablespoons
  vegetable oil
1½ teaspoons ground
  turmeric, plus extra
  to taste
1 teaspoon cumin
  seeds
2 onions, finely
  chopped
5-cm/2-in. piece of root
  ginger, peeled and
  finely chopped

2–4 green chillies/
  chiles, finely
  chopped
½ teaspoon chilli/chili
  powder
3 tomatoes, deseeded
  and chopped
½–1 teaspoon salt,
  or to taste
a handful of fresh
  coriander/cilantro
  leaves, to garnish

baking sheet, greased

SERVES 4–6

Preheat the oven to 220°C (425°F) Gas 7.

Pierce the aubergines/eggplants with a small knife and insert 2 garlic cloves and 1 clove into each. Drizzle the aubergines with 1–2 tablespoons of the oil and then dust with the turmeric. Roast for 10–15 minutes until the skin is well blackened.

Set aside to cool and discard the cloves. Roughly mash the aubergine/eggplant and garlic with a fork and set aside.

Heat the remaining 2–3 tablespoons oil in a deep-frying pan/skillet and add the cumin seeds, cook for 1 minute, then add the onions and cook for 5 minutes or until translucent and soft. Add the ginger and fresh chillies/chiles and cook for another 2 minutes, then add the mashed aubergine/eggplant mix, a pinch or 2 more of turmeric and the chilli/chili powder. Mix well and cook 20–25 minutes until the oil starts to separate.

Add the chopped tomatoes and salt, then gently simmer for 8–10 minutes until the tomatoes break down and the mixture is thick. Garnish with fresh coriander/cilantro and serve.

SUNIL'S DAL
KASHMIRI-STYLE RED BEAN DAL

3 tablespoons vegetable oil

2 very large onions (or 4 medium), thinly sliced

1 heaped tablespoon garam masala

1 heaped teaspoon ground cumin

7.5-cm/3-in. piece of root ginger, peeled and finely chopped

1 teaspoon Kashmiri (or mild) chilli/chili powder

1 teaspoon ground paprika

2 large mild red chillies/chiles, finely chopped

1–2 small hot green chillies/chiles, to taste, finely chopped (optional)

4 x 400-g/14-oz. cans red kidney beans, drained and rinsed

2–4 teaspoons salt, to taste, but be generous

a pinch of sugar

roughly chopped fresh coriander/cilantro leaves, to garnish

soft chapatis and/or steamed rice, to serve

SERVES 6

This recipe was inspired by an old friend, Sunil. He came from a family of amazing cooks, and would make his version of this dish as part of a North Indian feast, or thali (a large platter with lots of little dishes or compartments). After eating it at home in Manchester for years, I then came across a similar dish in Amritsar. The key to this dish is cooking it for a long time. It's the kind of dish you see bubbling away for hours in a Punjabi kitchen. But it is very quick to prepare, so I usually put this dish on first if I'm making a thali dinner.

Heat the oil in a large pan over medium heat and sweat the onions for 10 minutes or until softened and translucent. Add the garam masala and cumin, and cook for 3 minutes. Add the ginger, chilli/chili powder, paprika and fresh chillies/chiles, and fry gently for 5 minutes.

Add the kidney beans and 1.7 litres/7¾ cups water. Bring to the boil and season with salt to taste. It needs plenty of seasoning, so be generous. Add the sugar. Simmer for at least 2 hours – the longer the better to achieve a rich, thick gravy where the onions have completely cooked down into the sauce. Add more water if it gets too thick. Adjust the seasoning with more salt as necessary.

Garnish with fresh coriander/cilantro and serve with chapatis and/or steamed rice.

KHATTE CHOLE PURI

TEA-INFUSED CHICKPEAS WITH FRIED PURI BREAD

This is a classic street food recipe, and despite its simplicity it was one of our memorable eating experiences in India. We were waiting in Amritsar station for a train back to Delhi, as we were heading to Varanasi for Diwali. I watched the puri-wallah flatten his little puri dough balls and drop them into an enormous wok of oil where they puffed up into small balloon-like breads. We were mesmerized by him. He placed the bread in a bamboo bowl and filled it with the chickpea mixture. They were so delicious we all came back for more.

250 g/generous 1¾ cups '00' flour or wholemeal/whole-wheat flour, plus extra for dusting
½ teaspoon salt
2 tablespoons vegetable oil, plus extra for deep-frying

CHICKPEA FILLING
400 g/2⅓ cups dried chickpeas, soaked overnight and drained, or 2 x 400-g/14-oz. cans chickpeas, drained and rinsed
3 tea bags, such as Assam or other strong black tea
2 black cardamom pods (optional)
1 stick of cassia bark or cinnamon (optional)
1 tablespoon vegetable oil, plus extra for deep-frying
1 teaspoon cumin seeds
1 teaspoon ground coriander

4-cm/1½-in. piece of root ginger, peeled and chopped
1 onion, finely chopped
2 teaspoons garam masala
2 tablespoons tomato purée/paste
2 pinches of dried mango powder (amchoor)
½ teaspoon salt
thinly sliced red onion, sliced green chillies/chiles and fresh pomegranate seeds, to garnish

SERVES 4–6

First make the filling. If using dried chickpeas, place the drained chickpeas in a large heavy-based pan, cover with water and boil for 1½ hours until soft. Drain and rinse. Place the cooked or canned chickpeas in a heavy-based pan with the tea bags, cardamom and cassia bark or cinnamon, if using. Cover with water, bring to the boil and simmer for 1 hour.

Put the flour and salt in a bowl and add enough water (about 150 ml/⅔ cup) to make a soft dough. Dust the work surface with flour and knead the dough for 10 minutes. Grease the dough well, then place in a greased bowl, cover with clingfilm/plastic wrap and set aside in a warm place for 2 hours.

To finish the filling, add the oil to a deep frying pan/skillet or wok and fry the cumin seeds and ground coriander for 1 minute, then add the ginger and onion. Cook for 5 minutes, then add the garam masala and fry for a further 1–2 minutes.

Add 800 ml/3½ cups water, the tomato purée/paste, chickpeas, dried mango powder and salt. Mix well, bring to the boil and simmer for 10 minutes.

Meanwhile, heat 500 ml/2¼ cups vegetable oil in a deep-fryer or large pan. Knead the dough again, and make 12 balls the size of golf balls. Roll out each ball on a floured surface to about 15 cm/6 in. in diameter and no more than 5 mm/¼ in. thick.

Once the oil is smoking hot, carefully add the dough discs, in batches, and fry for 2 minutes on each side, until puffed up and golden. Remove with a slotted spoon and drain on paper towels. Ensure you allow the oil to heat again between batches.

Put a puri in a serving bowl, and add 2 spoonfuls of the chickpea mixture. Garnish with red onion, green chillies/chiles and fresh pomegranate seeds.

SPICED TOFU WITH SPINACH MASALA & PUMPKIN ROSTI

I wowed the critics with a version of this dish during MasterChef. The original dish was inspired by the classic crowd-pleaser, saag paneer. Using tofu works really well, as it takes on the flavours of cumin and mustard seeds during baking. This is ideal for Indian fusion dining at home. If you are making this a 'fine dining' plate, you can assemble it as a stack and decorate with edible flowers, such as violas or nasturtiums.

500 g/1 lb. 2 oz. baby spinach leaves
½ teaspoon salt
3 tablespoons vegetable or sunflower oil
500 g/1 lb. 2 oz. firm tofu, cut into 5 x 5 x 1-cm/ 2 x 2 x ½-in. slices
1 teaspoon black mustard seeds
1 teaspoon whole cumin seeds
1 small onion, thinly sliced
1 green chilli/chile, deseeded and finely diced
½ tablespoon ginger paste, or 2.5-cm/1-in piece of root ginger, peeled and grated
1 tablespoon garlic paste or crushed garlic cloves
2 tablespoons garam masala
18 cherry tomatoes, halved
100 g/3½ oz. creamed coconut block, mashed with 3 tablespoons warm water to form a smooth cream, or 100 ml/scant ½ cup coconut cream

ROSTI
1 small pumpkin or squash, peeled, deseeded and grated
1 large potato, grated
1 green chilli/chile, deseeded and finely diced
1 red chilli/chile, deseeded and finely diced
1 small bunch of fresh coriander/cilantro, finely chopped
2 tablespoons vegetable or sunflower oil
salt and freshly ground black pepper

TAMARIND GLAZE
2 tablespoons sugar
2 tablespoons red wine vinegar
100 g/3½ oz. tamarind concentrate/paste

SERVES 4

Preheat the oven to 180°C (350°F) Gas 4.

To make the rosti, place the grated pumpkin and potato in a large bowl. Add the chillies/chiles and the fresh coriander/cilantro, and season. Squeeze the mixture in a clean dish towel to remove excess water, then divide it into four patties and squeeze them between your palms to make firm patties.

Heat the oil in a frying pan/skillet over medium heat. Fry the patties on both sides for 3 minutes or until golden. Transfer to a baking sheet and put in the oven for 15 minutes or until cooked through.

Place the spinach in a pan and wilt over medium heat for 30 seconds. Blend using a food processor or blender to make a coarse purée, adding the salt and ½ tablespoon of the oil. Set aside.

Put the tofu slices in a shallow bowl and sprinkle over a little of the remaining oil and half the mustard and cumin seeds. Let marinate for 20–30 minutes. Heat the rest of the oil in a separate frying pan/ skillet. Fry the tofu slices in batches until golden brown. Drain on paper towels and keep warm.

Heat 2 tablespoons of the oil in a pan over medium heat and gently fry the onion for 5 minutes until softened and lightly coloured. Add the rest of the mustard and cumin seeds and fry for a few minutes. Add the chillies/chiles, ginger and garlic, and cook for 2–3 minutes. Add the garam masala and cook for 1 minute, then add the spinach purée and the tomatoes and cook for 3–4 minutes.

Put the tamarind glaze ingredients in a pan with a little water over high heat. Reduce by two-thirds. Strain. To serve, place a rosti on a plate, then add some spinach masala and several pieces of fried tofu. Drizzle with tamarind glaze and coconut cream.

From left to right: Train from Ooty to Coimbature, Tamil Nadu; Goats in Hampi, Karnataka; Banana seller at an old spice market.

South India

Our overland route took us from Mumbai down to Goa's beautiful beaches and Karnataka with its painted holy cows (all cows are holy in India, but the ones in Karnataka seem particularly revered). I have to be honest, we did enjoy some of the Western influences in Mumbai and Goa. We ate pasta for the first time in months and our shorts finally got an airing in Goa (finally expanding our sun tans from just our ankles and arms). We took the steam train over the Western Ghats to Tamil Nadu and finally down to Kerala, with its steamy backwaters and rather marvellous local newspapers.

The food in southern India is quite different from the north, and although we enjoyed the odd dosa in the northern regions, when we reached the southern regions, we became a little obsessed with all forms of Indian pancakes from masala dosas to ravi to oothapam, India's answer to the pizza perhaps (but don't tell Pema). Many of these dishes are naturally vegan and naturally gluten-free, but they are certainly not seen as a health food. Everyone seems to stop for a dosa around 4pm. It's not lunch or dinner. It's just dosa time. Most are served with the traditional combination of piping hot sambal (a Tamil-style thin dal) and coconut chutney. Most of the batters are easy to make, but some require a little forward planning for fermenting.

MYSORE MASALA DOSA
CRISPY PANCAKE WITH SPICED POTATO MASALA

I love all dosas, but there's a special place in my heart reserved for the masala dosa.
It's become much easier to find a good one when eating out nowadays. Perhaps it's
the two-day soaking and fermenting process that puts people off making them at home.
You can also buy dosa batter in some Asian grocery shops or delis – either dried or fresh,
or sometimes a homemade mixture in a little plastic bag. Ask at the counter – if they don't
sell it, they'll know someone who does. Play around with the fillings as much as you like.

300 g/1⅔ cups basmati
rice, rinsed and drained
100 g/generous ½ cup
split black urad dal
½ teaspoon fenugreek
seeds
1 teaspoon salt
vegetable oil, for frying
Spiced Coconut Chutney
(page 68) and Sambar
(page 63), to serve

FILLING
4 all-purpose potatoes,
such as Maris Piper/
Yukon gold
2 tablespoons vegetable
oil
1 teaspoon mustard
seeds
1 dried red chilli/chile,
crumbled

10 fresh or dried curry
leaves
1 onion, finely chopped
2 small green chillies/
chiles, finely chopped
2.5-cm/1-in. piece of root
ginger, peeled and
finely chopped, or 1
teaspoon ginger paste
¼ teaspoon chilli/chili
powder
¼ teaspoon ground
turmeric
30 g/¼ cup frozen peas
1 tablespoon cashew
nuts, broken into
pieces (optional)
¼–½ teaspoon salt,
to taste

MAKES 8–10

Put the rice in one bowl and the dal and fenugreek
seeds in another bowl, and add water to cover
by at least 5 cm/2 in. Soak for at least 6 hours
or overnight.

Drain the rice and dal mixtures, reserving
the drained liquid from both. Put the rice in a
food processor or blender and blitz until smooth,
adding 6–7 tablespoons of the soaking water,
or more if needed. Repeat with the dal mixture,
adding 5 tablespoons of the soaking water,
blending until smooth.

Put both mixtures in a large bowl. Mix together with
the salt and cover with clingfilm/plastic wrap. Leave
overnight in a warm place to ferment. The batter will
keep for up to a week in the fridge once it is
fermented, or can be frozen for up to six months.

Next day, make the filling. Boil the potatoes in
water to cover for 15 minutes or until tender, then
drain and mash. Set aside. Put the oil in a deep
frying pan/skillet or wok and add the mustard seeds,
dried red chilli/chile and curry leaves. Fry for a few
minutes, then add the onion, green chillies/chiles
and ginger, and cook for 7 minutes.

Add the chilli/chili powder and turmeric to the
pan and cook for 2 minutes, then add the mashed
potato, peas and cashews, if using, and mix
everything well. Season with the salt. Cover and
keep warm over a very low heat until needed.

Check the batter mix, and add enough cold
water to make a smooth pouring consistency. In a
large frying pan/skillet, add 1 tablespoon of oil and,
using a ladle, add 2–3 tablespoons batter to the
pan, then use the back of the ladle or a spoon to
smooth out the batter. Start in the centre and make
an outward spiral so that the batter reaches the
edge of the pan. Add a little more oil to the edges of
the pan to make sure that the pancake doesn't stick.
Cook for 2 minutes, then turn the pancake and cook
for a further 2–4 minutes until the edges are golden
brown and crispy. Transfer the pancake to a plate,
add some filling down the centre and fold in half.
Repeat to make remaining pancakes. Serve
immediately with coconut chutney and sambar.

SAMBAR
TAMIL DAL WITH VEGETABLE DRUMSTICKS

This Tamil Nadu dal is a classic South Indian recipe served with dosas and pancakes, or as part of a South Indian thali. You can buy a sambar masala mix from an Asian grocer (or you can make your own). The first time I had vegetable drumsticks (moringa), I was taken aback by the tough exterior, not realising the technique was to suck the sweet seeded middle out of this tube-like vegetable. It's unbelievably delicious, if a little messy, but this thin soup-like dal can be made with or without the drumsticks anyway.

200g/heaped 1 cup toor dal

200 g/7 oz. vegetable drumsticks (moringa), lightly scraped and cut into 6-cm/2½-in. pieces (optional)

1 teaspoon ground turmeric

1 teaspoon chilli/chili powder

4 green chillies/chiles, trimmed and slit in half lengthways

1 onion, finely chopped

2 tomatoes, chopped

1 teaspoon salt

1 tablespoon tamarind paste

a handful of fresh coriander/cilantro leaves, to serve

SAMBAR MASALA MIX

200 g/7 oz. dried red chillies/chiles

8 tablespoons coriander seeds

4 tablespoons cumin seeds

1½ tablespoons fenugreek seeds

1½ tablespoons black peppercorns

1½ tablespoons mustard seeds

2 teaspoons poppy seeds

2 sticks of cassia bark/cinnamon

a handful of curry leaves

2 teaspoons ground turmeric

2 teaspoons toor dal (unsoaked)

2 teaspoons channa dal (unsoaked)

TEMPERING

2 tablespoons vegetable oil

½ teaspoon cumin seeds

1 teaspoon coriander seeds

1 teaspoon black mustard seeds

15 fresh or dried curry leaves

¼ teaspoon asafoetida powder (hing)

SERVES 4–6

First, make the sambar masala spice mix. You will not need all of it, but you can store it in an airtight tub or jar for several months. In a hot frying pan/skillet, fry the dried chillies/chiles for 4–5 minutes, until crispy and starting to brown. Set aside. Toast the remaining sambar ingredients in same dry frying pan/skillet for 2–3 minutes, tossing gently so the spices do not burn. Add the chillies and grind using a pestle and mortar or food processor, to make a fine powder.

Put the toor dal in a bowl and cover with water. Leave to soak for 30 minutes, then drain and rinse. Pour 1.5 litres/6½ cups water into a large heavy-based pan and add the drumsticks, if using, the turmeric, chilli/chili powder, fresh chillies/chiles, onion, tomatoes and salt.

Bring to the boil and simmer for 20 minutes or until the toor dal is broken down and the drumsticks are cooked through. Add 1 tablespoon of the sambar masala mix and simmer for 6 minutes.

To make the tempering, heat the oil in a frying pan/skillet over medium heat and add all the tempering ingredients. Fry for 2–3 minutes until the spluttering stops, then pour this over the dal mixture. Add the tamarind paste and stir well. Add more water, if needed, to make a fairly thin consistency. Bring to a simmer again, stir in the fresh coriander/cilantro and serve.

OOTHAPAM

SOUTH INDIAN VEGETABLE CRUMPET

Oothapam is a thicker pancake than a dosa, made with semolina flour. The fermented version looks a bit like a crumpet, with fresh vegetables dropped into the batter as it cooks. People often say it looks like a pizza, but it doesn't taste like one. Its soft base is perfect for soaking up sambar (page 63), and I like to have an array of crunchy vegetable toppings. The traditional recipe is fermented for a few hours or overnight, but I've included a quick version that uses bicarbonate of soda/baking soda, so it's not as thick as the traditional version, but equally delicious.

vegetable oil, for frying
1–2 green chillies/chiles, to taste, thinly sliced
3 fresh or dried curry leaves, chopped
1 red onion, thinly sliced
2 tomatoes, finely chopped
1 carrot, grated
a small handful of chopped kale
Spiced Coconut Chutney (page 68) and Simple Sambal (page 33), or Sambar (page 63), to serve

TRADITIONAL BATTER
300 g/1⅔ cups basmati rice, rinsed until the water runs clear, then drained

100 g/generous ½ cup hulled whole urad dal
½ teaspoon fenugreek seeds
½ teaspoon salt

QUICK BATTER
300 g/2 cups coarse semolina flour
300 g/1⅓ cups plain soya/soy yogurt
1 teaspoon freshly squeezed lemon juice
1 teaspoon bicarbonate of soda/baking soda
1 teaspoon salt
pinch of asafoetida powder (hing)

MAKES 10–14

For the traditional fermented batter, put the rice in one bowl and the dal and fenugreek seeds in another bowl, and add water to cover by at least 5 cm/2 in. Soak for at least 6 hours or overnight.

Drain the rice and dal mixtures, reserving both the drained liquids. Put the rice in a food processor or blender and blitz until smooth, adding about 6–7 tablespoons of the soaking water, or more if needed. Repeat with the dal mixture, adding 5 tablespoons of the soaking water and blending until smooth.

Put both mixtures in a large bowl. Mix together with the salt and cover with clingfilm/plastic wrap. Leave overnight in a warm place to ferment. The batter will keep for up to 1 week in the fridge once it is fermented, or can be frozen for up to six months.

For the quick batter, mix all the ingredients together with enough water to make a thick pouring consistency. Set aside for 10–15 minutes. If using the fermented batter, add a little more water as necessary to make a thick pouring consistency.

Add ½ tablespoon oil to a large non-stick frying pan/skillet over medium heat. Using a ladle, spoon the batter into the centre of the pan and use the back of the ladle to smooth it out to the edges. Add a little oil around the edge to ensure it doesn't stick.

Quickly remove the pan from the heat and scatter the top of the pancake with some of the prepared vegetable topping ingredients. Use the back of the ladle to push the vegetables slightly into the batter. Return the pan to the heat and cook for 3 minutes or until it begins to brown underneath, then turn it over and cook for another 1–2 minutes. Repeat to make the remaining pancakes. Serve immediately with the suggested accompaniments.

GREEN JACKFRUIT VINDALOO

I really love a spicy curry, and vindaloo reminds me of curries in the UK. Before the 'lager culture' adoption of this dish, and making it as hot as possible, as a child I thought it was exotic and familiar at the same time. My parents had travelled a lot before they settled down to raise a family, and I remember my mum's vindaloo had pork and potatoes in it. I thought it was like meat and potatoes, but not. And although my mum had mistakenly made it far too hot, it was also delicious. I suspect a more authentic Parsi–Goan recipe would not include potatoes, and this penchant for a thick tomato sauce is very much a British curry thing.

I make this vindaloo-inspired curry with green jackfruit (and sometimes green papaya if I'm feeling flush). Green jackfruit is common across South India and Sri Lanka, as well as South-east Asia, and is often used in vegetarian curries because it has a great meaty and rather pork-like texture, so it might not be to every vegan's taste, but I love it and serve it on my street-food menu when I can. I buy it from an East Asian grocer, and I have never seen it fresh in its green state. Green papaya is easier to buy fresh but extraordinarily expensive. Both work exceptionally well, and the pickle-like spice base in this recipe can be used for other vegetable variations.

400 g/14 oz. waxy/red potatoes, peeled and cut into 2.5-cm/1-in. cubes
2 x 280-g/10-oz. cans green jackfruit, rinsed, drained and cut into 2.5-cm/1-in. pieces
1 teaspoon mustard seeds, toasted
1–2 tablespoons vegetable oil, for frying
3 onions, thinly sliced
20 fresh or dried curry leaves
1 teaspoon salt
½–1 teaspoon brown sugar
a handful of fresh coriander/cilantro leaves, to serve
steamed basmati rice and chapatis, to serve

SPICE PASTE
30 black peppercorns
10–20 large dried red chillies/chiles, depending on how hot you like it
1 teaspoon cumin seeds
8 cloves
5-cm/2-in. stick of cassia bark or cinnamon
1 star anise
2 tablespoons ginger paste, or 6-cm/2½-in. piece of root ginger, peeled and finely chopped
1 tablespoon vegetable oil
6 large garlic cloves, crushed
4 teaspoons red wine vinegar
1 tablespoon tamarind paste

SERVES 4–6

Boil the potatoes in water to cover for 10–12 minutes or until just tender, then drain and set aside.

Prepare the spice paste by mixing all the paste ingredients to a smooth mixture using a spice grinder or pestle and mortar. Grind the dry spices first, then blitz with the wet ingredients.

Place the cooked potatoes and prepared jackfruit in a large bowl and add half the spice paste along with the mustard seeds. Mix well and cover. Leave to marinate in the fridge for at least 1 hour.

Heat the oil in a large, heavy-based pan and cook the onions for 5 minutes or until softened, but not browned. Add the remaining spice paste, the marinated jackfruit and potatoes, and cook over medium heat for 5–6 minutes.

Add 800 ml/generous 3¼ cups water, the curry leaves, salt and sugar and bring to a simmer. Cook over low heat for 15 minutes, adding a little more water if necessary.

Garnish with fresh coriander/cilantro leaves and serve with rice and chapatis.

SPICED COCONUT CHUTNEY

This chutney, known as kobari pachadi, is eaten all over South India with pancakes and fried snacks. It will keep for three to four days in the fridge. You can omit the chilli/chile and add a pinch of cumin seeds instead, for a more fragrant, less-spiced version if you prefer. It's wonderful to be able to use fresh coconut, but desiccated coconut is more widely available and still tastes great.

100 g/1⅓ cups desiccated/dry unsweetened shredded coconut, or 200 g/7 oz. fresh coconut, shelled, peeled and finely grated
200 g/scant 1 cup plain soya/soy yogurt

TEMPERING
1 tablespoon vegetable oil
1 teaspoon mustard seeds
1 dried red chilli/chile, crumbled

MAKES 350 G/12 OZ.

If using desiccated/dried unsweetened shredded coconut, put it in a small bowl and add hot water to cover. Leave to soak for about 40 minutes. Drain and squeeze out the excess water. Put the fresh or soaked coconut in a food processor or blender and add the yogurt, then blend until smooth. Transfer to a serving bowl.

For the tempering, put the oil in a small frying pan/skillet over medium heat and add the mustard seeds and dried red chilli/chile. When the mixture starts to splutter, pour it over the coconut mixture and stir well to combine.

MANGO & LIME VEGETABLE SLAW

This zingy vegetable salad makes a great accompaniment to lots of spicy dishes, but mangoes and limes will always remind me of South India more than anywhere else in Asia. Serve this with any curry or spicy snack, or as part of a South Indian thali platter.

grated zest of 1 unwaxed lime and freshly squeezed juice of 4 limes
250 ml/heaped 1 cup mango pulp or purée
1 tablespoon tamari, or light soy sauce
¼ teaspoon salt, or to taste
1 teaspoon sugar (optional)

½ red cabbage, thinly sliced
½ white cabbage, thinly sliced
3 carrots, grated
a small handful of fresh mint leaves, finely chopped (optional)

SERVES 6

Put the lime zest and juice in a large bowl. Add the mango pulp to the bowl with the tamari, salt and sugar, if using – omit if the mango purée is sweetened. Whisk together. Ensure the sugar is dissolved, then check the seasoning.

Add the shredded vegetables to the bowl, and stir the dressing through to ensure everything is well coated. Stir in the mint and serve.

MAJJIGE HULI
KARNATAKAN VEGETABLES

Karnataka combines lush landscapes (home to tigers in some places apparently), blissed-out beaches (if slightly dangerous to swim in due to the currents) and mesmerizing ancient ruins. Our favourite was Hampi, a somewhat hippy enclave, with miles upon miles of boulder-strewn temples and ruins. There was a restaurant overlooking the river, where we enjoyed amazing food, such as this dish. It's traditionally made with sour curd or yogurt, but almond milk works well with a squeeze of lemon.

100 g/generous ½ cup split channa dal
50 g/⅔ cup desiccated/dry unsweetened shredded coconut, soaked in hot water, or ½ fresh coconut, shelled, peeled and grated
500 g/1 lb. 2 oz. gourd, such as doodhi/bottle gourd or ash gourd, peeled and cubed
200 g/7 oz. butternut squash, peeled, deseeded and cubed
2 potatoes, cubed
1 carrot, peeled and cubed
5-cm/2-in. piece of root ginger, peeled and grated, or 1 tablespoon ginger paste
1 tablespoon mustard powder
1 tablespoon freshly chopped coriander/cilantro leaves
10 fresh or dried curry leaves

2 green chillies/chiles, finely chopped
500 ml/2 cups almond milk
200 g/7 oz. green beans, trimmed
salt and freshly ground black pepper
freshly squeezed juice of ½ lemon, to serve
steamed basmati rice, and Mango and Lime Vegetable Slaw (page 68), to serve (optional)

TEMPERING
2 tablespoons vegetable oil
1 teaspoon mustard seeds
10 fresh or dried curry leaves
½–1 teaspoon chilli/chili powder, to taste
½–1 teaspoon salt, to taste

SERVES 4–6

Put the channa dal in a bowl and cover with water. Soak for 2 hours. Drain and rinse. Boil the channa dal in fresh water for 15–20 minutes, until soft. Drain and set aside. If using desiccated/dried unsweetened shredded coconut, put it in a bowl with hot water to cover. Soak for 30–40 minutes, then drain and squeeze out the excess water.

Put all the vegetables (except the green beans), in a large pan, add 300 ml/generous 1¼ cups water and a pinch of salt. Bring to the boil, then cover and simmer for 10–15 minutes until tender.

Drain the channa dal, and blend in a food processor or blender with 5 tablespoons water to make a smooth paste. Add the ginger to the blender with the mustard powder, soaked or fresh coconut, coriander/cilantro, curry leaves and chillies/chiles, then blend again until smooth.

Pour the almond milk into a large pan, mix in the spice paste and add the cooked vegetables. Bring to the boil, then add the green beans and simmer for 2–3 minutes, until cooked. Season to taste.

For the tempering, heat the oil in a small frying pan/skillet over medium heat and cook all the tempering ingredients until the spluttering stops. Pour over the vegetable curry, add a squeeze of lemon juice and stir well. Serve with rice and slaw.

RHUBARB SAMOSAS WITH A ROSE GLAZE

These samosas were one of my first dessert dishes on my street food menu. I love classic British desserts, and especially seasonal fruit like rhubarb. The flavours sing together in the crispy, sticky pastry.

800 g/1¾ lb. rhubarb, chopped into 2-cm/¾-in. pieces
4–6 tablespoons sugar, to taste
1½ teaspoons ground cinnamon
12 sheets of 30-cm/12-in. spring roll wrapper

coconut oil, melted, for brushing
2 teaspoons rose water
Star Anise & Vanilla Ice Cream, to serve

baking sheet, greased

SERVES 6

Preheat the oven to 120°C (250°F) Gas ½.

Put the rhubarb on two baking sheets and bake until the rhubarb has softened but has not fallen apart. Put the rhubarb in a bowl and add about 2–3 tablespoons of the sugar and the cinnamon. Stir well and check the flavour to ensure enough sugar has been added. Drain any excess liquid from the rhubarb into a small pan (to make sticky glaze later). Reduce the oven to 180°C (350°F) Gas 4.

Lay out a spring roll sheet and brush the edges with coconut oil (keep the other wrappers covered with a damp dish towel). Put 1 tablespoon of the rhubarb mixture in the bottom left corner of the sheet, then fold, lifting the corners to the edges until you have a well-wrapped triangle. Using a sharp knife, trim any excess edge, which will also help to seal the pastry. Repeat with the remaining wrappers.

Tip the remaining rhubarb and reserved juice into a small pan. Add 2–3 teaspoons sugar, to taste, and the rose water, and bring to the boil. Lower the heat and simmer gently until it is a sticky syrup. Strain.

Lay the pastries on the prepared baking sheet, and bake for 15–20 minutes until golden and crispy. Drizzle with the rose glaze just before serving. Serve with star anise and vanilla ice cream.

STAR ANISE & VANILLA ICE CREAM

This recipe uses coconut milk and coconut cream because they provide a thick, custardy base for the other flavours without being too intrusive. You can substitute with other vegan alternatives to dairy, but it will have a more sorbet-like texture. Only fat really gives ice cream its dreamy, creamy quality. The flavours of star anise and vanilla sit perfectly with the sticky rhubarb samosas opposite.

1 vanilla pod/bean, halved lengthways
½ teaspoon ground star anise seeds, extracted from the star anise
400 ml/1¾ cups canned coconut milk

160 ml/⅔ cup coconut cream, or separate the cream from the top of a can of coconut milk
3 tablespoons fruit syrup or agave syrup
100 g/½ cup sugar

SERVES 8–10

Using a knife, scrape all the seeds out of the vanilla pod/bean into a medium pan. Add all the remaining ingredients. Bring the mixture to a very gentle simmer over medium heat, so that the sugar is fully dissolved and the coconut is creamy and smooth.

Pour the mixture through a fine sieve into a bowl, then blend using a food processor or blender until smooth. Sieve again into a bowl, and cover the bowl with clingfilm/plastic wrap to prevent a skin forming.

Cool the mixture in the fridge. To use an ice cream maker, use the chilled mixture and follow the manufacturer's instructions. Transfer to a sealable freezerproof container and freeze.

To make in the freezer, transfer the chilled mixture to a shallow freezerproof container and freeze for 2 hours or until ice forms around the edges. Remove from the freezer and use a fork or an electric whisk to break up the crystals, then freeze for a further 2 hours and then whisk again. Leave to freeze until firm. Remove from the freezer 20 minutes prior to serving to soften.

MANGO & LIME SHERBET LASSI

You will need to make the lime sherbet two weeks in advance, and it can be used in other drinks and cocktails. You can omit the sherbet from the recipe or just add the juice of four limes instead to make it simpler, if you prefer.

500 ml/heaped 2 cups
    mango pulp or purée
2 tablespoons fruit syrup
    or agave syrup
    (optional)
400 g/1¾ cups plain
    soya/soy yogurt
400 g/14 oz. ice cubes,
    or 3 large handfuls

LIME SHERBET
juice of 16 limes
150 g/¾ cup caster/
    superfine sugar

SERVES 3–4

To make the lime sherbet, put the lime juice into a sterilized bottle with a sealable lid. Add the sugar and shake well. Leave on a windowsill for 2 weeks, shaking occasionally to dissolve the sugar. Open with care when ready to use.

Put the mango pulp in a food processor or blender and add the fruit syrup, if using – omit if the mango purée is sweetened. Add the yogurt, 100 ml/scant ½ cup of the lime sherbet and the ice, and blend until smooth. Pour into glasses and serve immediately.

BANANA & DATE LASSI

I was introduced to this combination by my great travel buddy Guy, who orders this whenever he gets the opportunity. There's a toffee-like quality to this lassi, and it's definitely one for those of you with a sweet tooth.

6 fresh dates, such as
    Medjool, stones/pits
    removed, or dried
    dates, soaked in boiling
    water for 30 minutes
3 bananas, peeled
600 ml/2½ cups plain
    soya/soy yogurt
1 tablespoon golden/light
    corn syrup (optional)
400 g/14 oz. ice cubes,
    or 3 large handfuls
ground cinnamon and
    black sesame seeds
    (optional), to serve

SERVES 3–4

Put the stoned dates, bananas, yogurt and syrup (if using) in a blender and add the ice. Blend until smooth. Pour into 3–4 glasses and serve immediately. Sprinkle some ground cinnamon and a pinch of black sesame seeds on top, if using.

Sri Lanka

When we arrived in Colombo, things felt a bit tense. Airport on high alert. Demonstrators and a significant army presence in the city. So we jumped on a train and headed for the hills. Sri Lankan trains are rickety, noisy and slow (and seat numbers don't count for anything so be prepared to be assertive about getting one). The rewards, however, are magnificent, travelling at this steady, almost wandering, pace through the most beautiful and lush landscapes in every shade and hue of green.

We loved our train journeys across Sri Lanka, and when we finally reached the east coast, we were met by more stunning landscapes and some barely explored beaches. Yala National Park sits on the far eastern corner of the island, and we stayed in the fishing village nearby. The people were hit hard by the 2003 tsunami and startling reminders remained all around: 7.5-m/25-ft sand banks and random boats sitting askew almost a mile inland, and hundreds of concrete floor plates of buildings that used to exist. Our local guide told us stories of that fateful day, and we were all deeply moved by the memorial on the beach. Sri Lanka is affected by several different monsoons, especially in the hill country.

KANDY

The town of Kandy sits on a plateau in these cool Sri Lankan hills in the Central Province, a great base from which to explore some of the surrounding temples, ancient palaces and holy sites (of which there are many). Kandy was the capital of former Kings and one of the most important places of pilgrimage for Buddhists, as it is home to the Temple of the Tooth (one of Gautama's actual teeth is purportedly kept here). I'd never really felt the urge to get married, but after seventeen years together (and a little persuasion from the children), we decided if we were going to get married then it would be right here in Kandy. We kept our promise to the children and returned three years later.

From left to right: Wedding flowers, Kundasale; Boys on train, Kandy to Ella; Sunrise on Kandy hillside; Golden Temple of Dambulla; Elephants playing in the river, Pinnawala Sanctuary; Stupa at Lankatilaka temple, Hiyarapitiya; Sunset on Kirinda beach.

POL SAMBOL
SRI LANKAN-STYLE COCONUT CHUTNEY

A little spicier than its Indian counterpart, I like to serve this alongside a cheela pancake or as part of a Sri Lankan dinner set.

100 g/1⅓ cups desiccated/dry unsweetened shredded coconut, or 200 g/7 oz. fresh coconut, shelled, peeled and finely grated
1 red onion, roughly chopped
10 fresh or dried curry leaves
freshly squeezed juice of 1 lemon or lime
2–4 red chillies/chiles, to taste, roughly chopped

SERVES 4–6

If using desiccated/dry unsweetened shredded coconut, put it in a bowl, add 100 ml/scant ½ cup boiling water and let soak for 15 minutes or until rehydrated and soft. Squeeze out the excess water.

Put the soaked or fresh coconut in a food processor or blender and add the remaining ingredients, except the chillies/chiles. Blend until finely chopped. Add the chopped chillies/chiles and store in the fridge for up to 5 days, where it will turn pink and get spicier over time.

KATTA SAMBOL
CHILLI/CHILE, TOMATO & ONION RELISH

I've learned to enjoy spicy food for breakfast these days and I like to add fresh tomato to this relish, to make it a little sweeter and more balanced. This is often served with Wedding Hoppers (page 88).

grated zest and freshly squeezed juice of 1 unwaxed lime
2 large red chillies/chiles, roughly chopped, or 1 tablespoon dried chilli/hot pepper flakes
a pinch of chilli/chili powder, to taste
1 red onion, roughly chopped
1 tomato, roughly chopped
salt, to taste

SERVES 4–6

Put the lime zest and juice in a bowl. Put the chillies/chiles, chilli/chili powder, onion and tomato into a food processor or blender and pulse together, or grind using a pestle and mortar.

Transfer to the bowl. Mix all the ingredients together, except for the salt, and leave for at least 1 hour before using. Add salt to taste before serving.

From left to right: Kotthu Parotta;
Parotta; Simple Sri Lankan Dal;
Katta Sambol; Pol Sambol.

PAROTTA
FLAKY ROTI BREAD

Parotta or roti is a soft and flaky layered fried bread found all over southern India and Sri Lanka. It can be served fresh with Sri Lankan dal or any gravy-like curry. You can make the parotta/roti, as below, to use in the Kotthu Parotta (see opposite), or use ready-made chapatis.

565 g/4¼ cups plain/
   all-purpose flour
1 teaspoon salt
1 teaspoon sugar

125 ml/½ cup sunflower
   or vegetable oil, plus
   extra to grease

MAKES 6–8

Mix the flour with the salt and sugar, then add enough cold water (about 300 ml/1¼ cups) to make a soft dough. Knead until soft, then add 1 tablespoon of the oil and knead for 10 minutes. Cover with a dish towel and let rest for 2 hours or overnight.

Grease the work surface with oil, then roll the dough into well-oiled balls, each about the size of a small orange. Roll each ball into a thick flatbread, 12 cm/5 in. across. Rest for 10 minutes, then stretch the bread as thinly as possible while continually smearing the dough with oil. It doesn't matter if the dough tears, but it's important to stretch it out as thinly as possible.

Fold the dough into a long pleated strip. Starting in the centre, form the strip into a spiral, then roll out gently to form a good-sized flatbread.

Heat a large frying pan/skillet or tawa over medium heat, and cook each parotta on both sides until golden brown. If you are eating the parotta with dal or curry, use your fingers to fluff up the cooked bread to separate the layers.

KOTTHU PAROTTA
SPICY FRIED ROTI WITH VEGETABLES

This is a classic Tamil street-food dish. Tamil food is mostly found in southern Indian and across Sri Lanka, and is well known for being super-spicy. The dish uses parotta, but you can use chapati just as easily. At the roadside cafés and stalls, the bread is chopped using two blunt metal blades, and you can hear this distinctive sound echoing from them. It's an adaptable dish – often served with meat and egg – but it can be made with a variety of vegetables, and you can also use leftover flatbreads.

3 parottas (opposite) or
   chapatis
1 tablespoon sunflower or
   vegetable oil
2.5-cm/1-in. piece of root
   ginger, peeled and
   finely chopped, or 1
   teaspoon ginger paste
1 teaspoon garlic paste
2 handfuls of diced
   vegetables, such as
   carrots, green beans,
   (bell) peppers, peas,
   courgettes/zucchini
1 onion, finely chopped
1 tomato, chopped

1–2 green chillies/chiles,
   to taste, finely chopped
1 teaspoon ground
   coriander
½ teaspoon chilli/chili
   powder
¼ teaspoon ground
   turmeric
½ teaspoon cumin seeds
½ teaspoon fennel seeds
2 tablespoons soy sauce
   or tamari
½ teaspoon lemon juice
salt, to taste

SERVES 4–6

Tear or chop the parotta or chapati into 2-cm/1-in. wide strips. Set aside. Heat the oil in a wok or large pan over high heat, then add the ginger and garlic paste and cook for 2–3 minutes. Add the diced vegetables, onion, tomato and fresh chillies/chiles, and cook for 3 minutes.

Add the remaining spices and mix well. Add the soy sauce and cook for 5–6 minutes, until the tomatoes are completely soft and the vegetables are well cooked, then add the bread strips and stir over high heat ensuring all the bread is well coated.

Remove the wok from the heat, add the lemon juice, check the seasoning and add salt as required. Serve immediately.

SIMPLE SRI LANKAN DAL
CREAMY LENTIL & COCONUT DAL

Almost six months into our trip, some friends from home joined us for a two-week tour of Sri Lanka. One of my favourite places was a village in the hills called Ella. We filled our days with easy-going walks, tea plantations and breathtaking views before returning to our guesthouse with hiking-fuelled appetites. We ate this dal with almost every meal in Sri Lanka. It has a lightly spiced tempering and is creamy with thick coconut milk. It's a great side dish as part of a dinner or a filling snack with chapati.

180 g/1 cup red lentils
½–1 teaspoon salt, to taste
1 teaspoon ground turmeric
2 tablespoons thick coconut milk (use the creamy part of the unshaken can)
1 large tomato, chopped
bread or steamed rice, to serve

TEMPERING

1 tablespoon sunflower or vegetable oil
1 onion, finely chopped
½ teaspoon mustard seeds
½ teaspoon cumin seeds
½ teaspoon fenugreek seeds
15 fresh or dried curry leaves
1–2 green chillies/chiles, to taste, finely chopped

SERVES 4

Put the lentils in a pan and add 700 ml/3 cups of water, the salt and turmeric. Bring to the boil and simmer until the lentils are just cooked. Using a large spoon, skim off any foam and residue. Add the coconut milk and chopped tomato, then simmer for 3 minutes or until fully cooked. Check the seasoning and add more salt if needed.

For the tempering, heat the oil in a small frying pan/skillet over medium heat and fry the onion gently for 5–10 minutes until translucent and starting to turn golden brown. Add the mustard, cumin and fenugreek seeds, curry leaves and chillies/chiles. Cook for 4–5 minutes more. Pour the tempering over the dal and serve with your choice of bread or rice.

MASALA CHAI
INDIAN SPICED TEA

I didn't fall in love with masala chai (Indian spiced tea) the first time I drank it. I felt it went against my preferred British tea-drinking, which was builder's black without sugar. I soon realized I would be forfeiting any tea-drinking while travelling if I didn't at least try to like it. Everywhere we stopped across India and Sri Lanka, there was always a chai-wallah (chai is simply the name for tea and wallah is the seller). After a few months, I found myself hankering for this fragrant and sweet pick-me-up, especially after endless hours on the road. Being woken by the chai-wallah's calls on the overnight train from Varanasi has long stuck in my memory, and my husband and I still call out to each other 'chai-di-chai' if we're making a brew.

6 tea bags
seeds of 4–5 green cardamom pods, to taste, crushed
1 teaspoon fennel seeds
1 large piece of cassia bark or cinnamon
a pinch of ground black pepper
2 cloves (optional)
2-cm/1-in. piece of root ginger, peeled and thinly sliced
sugar, as needed
soya/soy milk or cream, to serve (optional)

MAKES A POT OF TEA FOR 4–6 PEOPLE

Boil 300 ml/1¼ cups water in a small pan and add the tea bags. Toast the cardamom and fennel seeds in a separate dry pan over medium heat for 30 seconds, stirring occasionally. Finely grind the dry spices (cardamom and fennel seeds, cassia bark, black pepper and cloves, if using) in a spice blender or using a pestle and mortar.

Add 2 teaspoons of ground spice mixture to the pan with slices of fresh ginger. Bring to the boil and simmer for 5–10 minutes. Add 1 teaspoon sugar per person, then use a tea strainer to pour the tea into cups. You can add soya/soy milk or cream, for a more authentic creamy chai.

SPRING VEGETABLE CHEELA
GRAM FLOUR PANCAKE WITH PEAS AND LEEKS

Cheela is a savoury gram-flour pancake that often contains chopped vegetables. For speed, you can use ground instead of whole spices, but halve the quantities specified. However, you should still toast the spices.

2 tablespoons cumin
    seeds
1 tablespoon coriander
    seeds
350 g/2¾ cups gram flour
2 teaspoons baking
    powder
1 teaspoon salt
1 teaspoon black pepper
2 spring onions/scallions,
    thinly sliced diagonally
a large handful of fresh
    coriander/cilantro
    leaves, chopped, plus
    extra sprigs to garnish
vegetable oil, for frying
3 baby leeks, thinly sliced
100 g/⅔ cup peas

PINEAPPLE CHUTNEY
20 g/¼ cup desiccated/
    dry unsweetened
    shredded coconut
150 g/¾ cup freshly
    chopped pineapple
    or canned pieces
1 small red chilli/chile,
    finely chopped
a squeeze of lime juice

MAKES 8–10

Toast the cumin and coriander seeds in a dry frying pan/skillet over medium heat for 30 seconds, stirring occasionally, to release the aroma. Finely grind the toasted spices in a spice blender or using a pestle and mortar.

Sift the gram flour and baking powder into a large bowl, then add the spices, salt, pepper and 570 ml/2½ cups water. Whisk to form a batter, then set aside for 30 minutes.

To make the pineapple chutney, rehydrate the coconut in boiling water for 10–15 minutes. Squeeze out any excess water and mix the coconut with the pineapple, chilli/chile and lime juice.

Stir the spring onions/scallions and coriander/cilantro into the batter. Heat 1–2 tablespoons oil in a small or medium frying pan/skillet and add a small handful of the sliced leeks and peas. When the leeks start to soften, pour over the batter mixture and cook the pancake for 4–5 minutes or until golden underneath, then turn it over and cook the other side for 4–5 minutes or until golden. Set aside each pancake on paper towels to drain and then place in a low oven to keep warm until ready to serve.

Repeat with the remaining leeks, peas and batter mixture to make 8–10 pancakes. Serve immediately, with the pineapple chutney.

BLACK CURRY WITH BEETROOT & SPINACH

We enjoyed a variation of this curry at our jungle retreat in Kitulgala, in the Sabaragamuwa province. Our host was a giant of a man with a beard and moustache to match. In-between rafting and exploring the cloud-forest mountains, we were served fabulous vegan banquets. There are different variations of curry in Sri Lanka, often mild and creamy with lots of coconut milk or deep red and spicy with ground chillies/chiles and tomato. This recipe is a more unusual black curry with roasted whole spices.

2–4 dried red chillies/
    chiles, to taste
550 g/1¼ lb. raw
    beetroot/beets,
    unpeeled, or peeled
    cooked beetroot/beets,
    but not in vinegar
2 red onions, finely
    chopped
1 tablespoon garlic paste
1 lemongrass stalk
2 teaspoons cumin seeds
2 teaspoons coriander
    seeds
1 teaspoon fennel seeds
4 tablespoons vegetable
    oil
300 g/11 oz. frozen or
    fresh spinach, or
    drained and rinsed
    canned spinach
300 ml/generous 1¼ cups
    vegetable stock
300 ml/generous 1¼ cups
    coconut milk
120 g/1 cup cashew nuts
salt and freshly ground
    black pepper
steamed rice, to serve

SERVES 4–6

Put the chillies/chiles in a bowl and cover with hot water. Leave to soak for 30–40 minutes. Drain.

If you are using raw beetroot/beets, put them in a pan of boiling water and simmer for 1 hour, then leave them to cool in the liquid. Once cooled, drain and then peel the skin from the beetroot/beets using your fingers. Chop into bite-sized pieces.

Using a food processor, blend the onions, garlic paste, soaked chillies and lemongrass to a smooth paste. Set aside.

Toast the cumin, coriander and fennel seeds in a dry pan over medium heat for 30 seconds, stirring occasionally, to release the aroma. Finely grind the spice mixture using a spice grinder or a pestle and mortar.

Heat the oil in a pan over high heat and add the onion paste. Cook for 3–4 minutes, then add the spice paste and mix well. Reduce the heat to medium and cook, stirring continuously, for 10 minutes, then add the chopped beetroot/beets and spinach, and cook over medium heat for 2 minutes.

Add the stock and simmer for 8–10 minutes. Add the coconut milk and bring to the boil, then gently simmer for 3 minutes. If the curry starts to get too dry, add a little more water. Season generously with black pepper and add salt to taste.

Toast the cashew nuts in a dry pan over medium heat for 1–2 minutes, stirring occasionally, until golden, then scatter them over the curry. Serve with rice.

WEDDING HOPPERS
FERMENTED COCONUT PANCAKES

These are not really called wedding hoppers, just rice hoppers. But in Sri Lanka it's traditional to eat them for your wedding breakfast, which is when we first tried them. At that point we hadn't had the greatest experiences with vegetarian Sri Lankan food, but then we stayed with Parlita and his family. His staff served us an enormous vegan Sri Lankan banquet for our wedding dinner. The next morning, these delicate-looking rice-batter baskets were served with an egg in the bottom, and some super-hot chilli/chile and onion relish. They are very similar to the South Indian-style pancakes called appam, but the hopper's wafery crispy edges, with a gooey middle, perhaps explain why this dish is such a popular snack. It's often eaten at breakfast, so you can leave the batter to ferment overnight. The wok should be no bigger than 15 cm/6 in., or the hopper will lose its shape when it comes out of the pan. I often serve them with raspberry jam at home, or Katta Sambol (page 78) if I'm in the mood for a spicy breakfast.

1½ teaspoons active dried yeast
2 tablespoons granulated/white sugar
240 ml /1 cup coconut milk
360 g/2¾ cups rice flour
a pinch of salt
1–2 tablespoons vegetable oil
raspberry jam/jelly or Katta Sambol (page 78), to serve

15-cm/6-in. wok with a lid

SERVES 4–6

Put the yeast in a bowl and sprinkle over 2 tablespoons warm water, mix well and add 1 tablespoon of the sugar. Set aside for 10 minutes or until frothy.

Pour coconut milk into a bowl and add 185 ml/¾ cup warm water. Add this to the frothy yeast mixture.

Sift the rice flour into a bowl and add the remaining sugar and the salt, then slowly stir in the yeast and coconut mixture. This should form a thick, smooth pancake-like batter. Cover and leave to stand for 4–6 hours or overnight if possible.

Using paper towels rub oil over the wok. Place over medium heat.

Add a little more water to the batter mixture, to ensure a smooth and pourable, but medium-thick, batter. Once the pan is hot, reduce the heat and, using a ladle, add one scoop of batter to the pan, and immediately swirl it around the wok, right up the side. Cook for 5–8 minutes. The edges should be thin and crispy, and the bottom a little gooey and soft. You are aiming to create a thin and crisp dome-shaped pancake (hopper).

Use a flexible spatula to carefully remove the hopper from the pan. Repeat with the remaining batter until used up. Serve warm with a big dollop of raspberry jam or katta sambol.

COCONUT & LIME SORBET

This sorbet is more like an ice cream because of the creamy coconut milk. I often keep a tub in the freezer to serve with fruit-based desserts and tarts.

150 ml/scant ⅔ cup agave syrup
grated zest of 1 unwaxed lime and the juice of 4 limes
400 ml/1¾ cups coconut milk

Caramelized Pineapple (opposite), to serve

MAKES ABOUT 1 LITRE/QUART

To make the sorbet, put 100 ml/scant ½ cup water in a small pan and add the agave syrup and lime zest. Bring to a gentle boil, then remove from the heat and leave to cool.

Put the coconut milk in a large bowl and add the lime juice and cooled zest mixture. Whisk together to combine. To use an ice cream maker, use the chilled mixture and follow the manufacturer's instructions. Transfer to a sealable freezerproof container and freeze. To make in the freezer, transfer the chilled mixture to a shallow freezerproof container and freeze for 2 hours or until ice forms around the edges. Use a fork or an electric whisk to break up the crystals, then freeze for 2 hours and whisk again. Leave to freeze until firm.

Remove from the freezer 20 minutes prior to serving to allow the ice cream to soften. Serve with the caramelized pineapple.

CARAMELIZED PINEAPPLE

One of my favourite memories of travelling with my family in Asia is eating exotic fruits as if they were apples. The children's favourite was pineapple.

1 tablespoon liquid glucose, or a pinch of cream of tartar
200 g/1 cup golden caster/granulated sugar
185 ml/¾ cup coconut milk, at room temperature

40 g/¼ cup skinned pistachio nuts, chopped (optional)
1 pineapple
Coconut & Lime Sorbet (opposite), to serve

SERVES 8–10

To make the caramel, put 60 ml/¼ cup water in a heavy-based pan with the glucose and sugar. Stir to help dissolve the sugar, then gently bring to a simmer over medium heat. It is important not to stir the mixture, just swirl the pan occasionally. Heat until the mixture is clear, then turn up the heat slightly and simmer for 10–15 minutes, until it is deep brown (but not burnt). Remove from the heat, then carefully whisk in the coconut milk – it will splutter so take care. The caramel is served warm but can be refrigerated in a glass bottle for up to a month and reheated.

If using pistachios, preheat the oven to 180°C (350°F) Gas 4. Scatter the chopped pistachios over a baking sheet and roast for 5 minutes until slightly browned. Transfer to a bowl and leave to cool.

Using a sharp knife, cut the top and bottom off the pineapple, then stand it on one end and cut off the peel and the 'eyes' (cut with a sharp knife from either side, making a small V cut following the diagonal line of eyes). Cut the pineapple into thick slices, then cut out the central core. Gently reheat the caramel sauce in a small pan over a medium-low heat until warm, if prepared in advance.

Heat a ridged griddle over high heat then quickly cook the pineapple for 5–7 minutes on each side, until lightly golden. Place on serving plates, drizzle with caramel sauce and scatter over the toasted pistachios. Serve with the coconut and lime sorbet.

BANANA PANCAKES VENDOR-STYLE

No traveller's recipes would be complete without a recipe for the ubiquitous banana pancake, sold across the Indian subcontinent and South-east Asia. The recipe lands here because we ate a lot of these pancakes when we were in Sri Lanka. Vegetarian and vegan food was sometimes hit and miss for us in Sri Lanka, so banana pancakes became our trusted go-to snack. The authentic vendor-style is not made with egg, but a sweetened roti dough. According to the children, the full experience must also incorporate peanut butter and chocolate spread, whereas my dear travel friend Natalie would insist it was all wrong without condensed milk. You can use ready-made roti if you want to save time.

270 g/2 cups plain/
   all-purpose flour
1–2 teaspoons sugar,
   to taste
½ teaspoon salt
150 ml/⅔ cup vegetable
   oil, plus extra to grease
2–3 ripe bananas, peeled
   and thickly sliced
vegan chocolate spread
   (optional)
peanut butter (optional)
soya/soy cream, golden/
   light corn syrup or
   home-made caramel
   (page 91), to serve

MAKES 4

Put the flour in a bowl and add the sugar and salt. Mix together well, then add enough cold water to make a soft dough (about 150 ml/⅔ cup). Knead until soft, then add 1 tablespoon of the oil and knead for a good 10 minutes. Cover the dough with a damp dish towel and leave to rest for at least 2 hours.

Grease the work surface with oil, then roll out the dough into well-oiled balls about the size of golf balls. Roll out each ball to make a flatbread about 12 cm/4½ in. in diameter. Leave to rest for 10 minutes.

Take each flatbread and, using your hands, stretch the dough as thinly as possible while continually smearing the dough with oil. It doesn't matter if the dough tears, but it's important to stretch it out thinly. Fold the dough back over itself in layers, to make a rough square about 10 cm/4 in. wide. Roll the dough out as thinly as possible to fit your largest frying pan/skillet.

Heat the frying pan/skillet, or a tawa, over medium heat and cook the pancake on one side (do not cook it too much at this stage, as it will make it difficult to fold the pancake), then turn it over and add some of the banana, chocolate spread or peanut butter, if using, into the centre, filling about half the pancake.

Fold in the sides of the pancake to form a thick rectangle, then cook gently on all sides until golden brown and the sweet dough is well cooked, adding more oil if necessary. Drain for 1–2 minutes on paper towels. Repeat with the remaining dough balls. Slice each pancake in half at an angle, then serve drizzled with soya/soy cream, golden/light corn syrup or home-made caramel for an extra sweet hit.

THAILAND, LAOS & VIETNAM

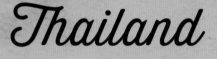

Thailand

Thailand is the first Asian country we ever landed in back in the early nineties. It's also where we chose a test trip with four-year-old twins, prior to our gap year. It's such an easy country to travel in, even twenty years ago. The sleeper trains are phenomenal and proved a great adventure for the children. And it's very simple to link journeys together with cheap air conditioned bus routes and the famous songthaews, shared taxis that consist of a pick-up truck holding two facing benches in the back, with a roof. The record I've seen on one of these was twenty people and a broken down motorbike, when we spent a week travelling a more remote border route near Burma.

It's still possible to explore less developed places in the north of the country, whereas the south has reached unrivalled popularity for its picture-perfect islands and beaches. The crowds are hard to escape these days, but with national park gems like Khao Sok, Similan and Taratao, for me it will always be a country worth exploring further.
I just love Thai cities too. My personal favourite is Hat Yai, with its morning markets of produce heaven and consistently good street food that mixes up Thai, Malay and Muslim food. For the children, it's always Bangkok.

BANGKOK "Ahhh the smell of Bangkok, there's nothing like it!" my seven-year-old son Tevo once declared. Stepping out of Bangkok airport is like walking into a slightly swampy-smelling steam room. In a good way we think. Bangkok is a huge place. Dense and sprawling at the same time, not unlike London, which is of a similar size and population. But it feels a million miles away. We always try to stay in different parts of the city to explore places we've never been before. But the smell is always the same. A background of slight decay, wafting distant memories of the swamp it once was, overlaid with the powerful combining aromas of incense and street food. There are so many things we have fallen in love with in this city. Street food is very much one of them, and certainly transformed my passion for food into something that inspired me. It's also where my son fell in love with Pad Thai or Phat Thai Jay, which is the vegetarian version, Jay meaning vegetarian in Thai. Obviously a word we learned fairly early on, in an effort to avoid the ubiquitous fish sauce. I'm not sure how successful that endeavour was though.

From left to right: Bamboo hut; Fishing boats, Pak Bara; Huts on stilts, Koh Lipe; Children on rope swing, Koh Rawi; Reclining Buddha, Wat Po, Bangkok; Buddha statues, Wat Po, Bangkok; Sunset view across Taratao National Marine Park.

PAD THAI JAY
VEGETARIAN THAI FRIED NOODLES

My recipe is based on my son's favourite pad Thai trader on Rambuttri Soi (with a few insights from my best friend Natalie on that elusive secret ingredient). I don't include garlic, because, for me, this seems a European influence and it slightly overpowers the balance of sweet and salty, and hot and sour. This classic Thai flavour balance is perfectly represented in a good pad Thai. I'm not sure why, but many European versions strike me as too sweet and lacking in the sour–salty notes that raise the game of this simple noodle dish. And the secret ingredient? That would be some radish pickle juice. It has a slightly funky unique odour, and it is the subtle sour note that hits the spot with a great pad Thai.

120 g/4 oz. dried, flat rice noodles 5 mm–1cm/¼–½ in. wide
2 tablespoons vegan fish sauce (page 13), vegetarian Worcestershire sauce or extra soy sauce and salt to taste
5–6 tablespoons light soy sauce, to taste
¼ teaspoon fine salt
3–4 tablespoons soft brown sugar, or to taste
3 tablespoons tamarind pulp, or 1 tablespoon tamarind concentrate
2 tablespoons pickle juice from Pickles (page 141), or rice vinegar
50 g/heaped ⅓ cup unsalted peanuts
1 tablespoon groundnut/peanut oil or vegetable oil

200 g/7 oz. firm tofu, rinsed, drained and crumbled
6 mangetouts/snow peas, thinly sliced lengthways
2 shallots, thinly sliced
50 g/1 cup beansprouts
a small handful of fresh coriander/cilantro leaves, roughly chopped
2 large red chillies/chiles, finely chopped
1 lime, quartered and then halved

SERVES 2

Put the noodles in a bowl and cover with hand-hot water. Leave to soak for 30 minutes or until softened but still with lots of bite. Drain in a colander. Set aside.

Put the vegan fish sauce (if using) in a jug/pitcher and add the soy sauce, salt, sugar, tamarind and pickle juice. If not using vegan fish sauce or Worcestershire sauce, you will need to add extra soy sauce and salt to taste. Add 2 tablespoons water, and stir well until the sugar is fully dissolved. Taste the mixture; it should be salty, sweet and sour all at the same time. Add more sugar, tamarind, pickle juice, rice vinegar or soy sauce as needed.

Toast the peanuts in a dry pan over medium heat for 1–2 minutes, stirring occasionally, until golden. Chop roughly and set aside.

Heat a wok or a large pan over high heat, add the oil and gently fry the tofu for 8–10 minutes, until crispy and golden. Add the mangetouts/snow peas and shallots and stir-fry for 30 seconds more.

Add the noodles to the wok along with 80 per cent of the liquid mixture. Cook over high heat for 1 minute, then add half the beansprouts. Mix everything together, then add the remaining liquid. The noodles should be moist and sticky. Serve immediately in a large bowl, topped with the remaining beansprouts, the coriander/cilantro, peanuts and a sprinkle of chopped chillies/chiles. Serve with a squeeze of lime.

PAD KA PRAO
HOLY BASIL WITH AUBERGINE/EGGPLANT

One of the truly classic and simple Thai dishes of all time is stir-fried holy basil. Try not to skimp on using the correct basil, as European basils are just not quite right. The best version of this dish I have ever eaten was in Phitsanulok night market, a town that sits at the central crossroads for all the produce from the hugely rural north and central provinces. The dish is all about this uniquely flavoured herb, and the fresher it is the better. Whereas most Thai menus will offer ka prao (holy basil) dishes with pork or chicken, it's not difficult to find this version with aubergine/eggplant. Thais love aubergine/eggplant. Its meaty texture stands up to the powerful flavour of the holy basil. This is a simple, quick stir-fry supper.

1 tablespoon peanut/
   groundnut oil or
   vegetable oil
1 aubergine/eggplant,
   halved lengthways and
   cut into 5-mm/¼-in.
   diagonal slices
4 garlic cloves, crushed
4 spring onions/scallions,
   sliced diagonally
2 large red chillies/chiles,
   thinly sliced diagonally

3–4 tablespoons light
   soy sauce, to taste
2 tablespoons vegetarian
   oyster sauce
2 tablespoons dark sweet
   soy sauce, or to taste
25 holy basil leaves
steamed rice and Nam
   Prik Pao (opposite),
   to serve

SERVES 2

Heat the oil in a large frying pan/skillet over medium-high heat, then add the aubergine/eggplant and stir-fry until starting to brown on each side. Add the garlic, spring onions/scallions and chillies/chiles. Fry for a further 2 minutes, then add all the remaining ingredients, except the holy basil.

Cook for 2 minutes, then remove from the heat. Check the seasoning and adjust to taste. Off the heat, add the holy basil leaves and stir until they have wilted. Serve with steamed rice and a spoonful of nam prik pao on the side.

NAM PRIK PAO
THAI CHILLI/CHILE JAM

This sweet, fiery and sticky roasted chilli/chile paste is much loved across Thailand and an important component to many classic Thai dishes (or added to a sandwich). I base my recipe on David Thompson's, but without the shrimps and fish sauce. While it is more traditional to roast the chillies/chiles, garlic and shallots, frying them brings an added depth to the flavour. This incredibly versatile sauce can be used in all manner of stir-fries, salads and soups.

500 ml/2 cups vegetable
   oil
60 g/2¼ oz. garlic cloves,
   thinly sliced
120 g/4 oz. red shallots,
   thinly sliced
60 g/2¼ oz. dried red
   chillies/chiles, soaked
   in boiling water for
   20 minutes, deseeded,
   if you prefer, chopped

6 tablespoons tamarind
   pulp, or 2 teaspoons
   tamarind concentrate
200 g/1 cup soft brown
   sugar
4 tablespoons vegan fish
   sauce (page 13), tamari
   or vegetarian
   Worcestershire sauce

MAKES 750 ML/3 CUPS

To make the chilli/chile jam, heat the oil in a pan over medium heat and cook the garlic until crispy and brown. Remove from the pan, using a slotted spoon, and fry the shallots in the same way. Remove from the pan and set aside. Fry the chillies/chiles in the same way. If using tamarind concentrate, dissolve it in a small bowl with 100 ml/scant ½ cup water. Set aside.

Put the chillies/chiles in a mortar (or food processor) and add the garlic and shallots. Grind or blend to a paste, adding 60 ml/¼ cup of the frying oil. Pour the mixture into a small pan.

Cook over medium heat for 2 minutes, then add all the remaining ingredients. Simmer gently for about 20 minutes or until you have a thick, jam-like sauce, stirring occasionally. Be careful that it doesn't burn. The oil will separate a little on the surface – there's no need to remove it. Store the jam in a sterilized screwtop jar for up to 1 month in the fridge.

STICKY BBQ TOFU SKEWERS

We have had many stopovers in Bangkok over the years, where we have filled our days wandering around the streets and markets, visiting temples, eating and joining in celebrations. It's a great city: vibrant, diverse and colourful. On our first visit to Thailand with the children when they were four, they were less than impressed by some of the smells and the heat. But after six months in India and Sri Lanka, they found it relatively clean and well kept when we returned. That doesn't mean that it is. What many tourists don't see when they visit Bangkok are the acres of slums that exist along riversides and railway lines. How someone emerges from this squalor wearing a perfectly pressed white T-shirt still amazes me to this day.

One of my favourite celebrations in Thailand is the King's birthday on December 5th, when thousands of people take to the streets with their little candles. We ate some incredible street food that night, wandering around the Thieves Market. The most memorable was a skewer of sticky, spicy barbecued tofu with a banana leaf filled with sticky rice for mopping up a nutty, sweet–sour–salty dressing. This recipe is from my street food menu, which I serve with sticky rice and Mango & Lime Vegetable Slaw (page 68).

6 large fresh red chillies/chiles, finely chopped or 6 large dried red chillies, or 2 tablespoons Nam Prik Pao (page 101)
6 garlic cloves, finely chopped, or 1 tablespoon garlic paste
2.5-cm/1-in. piece of root ginger, peeled and finely chopped, or 1 tablespoon ginger paste
½ teaspoon ground white pepper
2 tablespoons cooking Sherry or Shaoxing
2 tablespoons vegan fish sauce (page 13, optional)
2 tablespoons dark soy sauce
4 tablespoons agave syrup
1 tablespoon soft brown sugar
½ bunch of fresh coriander/cilantro, leaves and stems chopped
36 tofu puffs
sea salt
Peanut & Cucumber Dipping Sauce (page 116), to serve
Nam Prik Pao (page 101), to serve (optional)
sticky rice, to serve (optional)

12 bamboo skewers
baking sheet, greased

SERVES 4–6

Soak the bamboo skewers in cold water. If using dried chillies/chiles, put them in a bowl and cover with hot water. Leave them to soak for 30 minutes, then, wearing gloves, squeeze out the excess liquid. Chop the chillies/chiles.

In a large bowl, add the chopped fresh or soaked chillies and all the remaining ingredients, except the tofu puffs. Mix well until all the sugar has dissolved. Check the seasoning and add salt to taste.

Put the tofu puffs in the bowl and stir to coat in the marinade. Set aside for at least 1 hour or preferably overnight.

Preheat the grill/broiler to high. Skewer 3 pieces of puff onto each bamboo skewer. Lay the skewers on the prepared baking sheet and put under the grill/broiler. Grill/broil, turning occasionally, for 10–12 minutes or until golden brown and crispy on the outside. Serve two or three skewers per person with a little pot of peanut and cucumber dipping sauce and some nam prik pao. You can also serve them with sticky rice.

From left to right: Salsify & Chilli Fritters;
Nam Prik Pao; Kanom Jin Nahm Prik Tofu;
fresh watercress, cucumber and chillies/chiles.

KANOM JIN NAHM PRIK TOFU
SMOKY TOFU & CHILLI/CHILE JAM WITH KANOM JIN NOODLES

I'm a huge fan of David Thompson, an Australian chef and writer whose depth of knowledge in Thai cuisine is unsurpassed. His beautiful and slightly complicated Thai Street Food is inspiring to read. By the time you read this, we will also have had the joy of visiting his restaurant in Bangkok, called Nahm. I use his books to help me understand the basis of many traditional recipes and techniques in Thai food. His recipe for prawns/shrimp and chilli/chile jam (kanom jin nahm prik) was the inspiration for this dish, and my smoky tofu version was runner-up in Best Main at the British Street Food Awards in 2012. I lost out to fish and chips by one point in the voting. Not bad for a vegan dish facing a British audience, I think!

The recipe has a number of component parts, and I suggest making your batch of Thai chilli/chile jam (Nam Prik Pao, page 101) at least a day beforehand. It will make the recipe feel less daunting, and, of course, you can make the chilli/chile jam simply in its own right, so it's ready to use in lots of Thai recipes, or as a simple stir-fry sauce or dip. Another ingredient that is useful to prepare earlier is some vegan fish sauce (keep a stock bottle for your Southeast Asian fish-free cooking, page 13). If you prefer, you can substitute the chilli/chile jam by roasting 5 fresh red chillies and adding those to the paste.

The deep-fried whole bird's eye chillies/chiles can be a little intimidating at first, but their notably fierce heat is tempered by the frying process and leaves a deep and smoky chilli/chile flavour that has to be tried at least once. These cheeky little additions are often served alongside dishes in Thailand and Laos, so people can adjust the heat of what they're eating to suit their own taste.

100 g/3¾ oz. creamed coconut, dissolved in 100 ml/scant ½ cup hot water, or 100 ml/scant ½ cup coconut cream
1 teaspoon tamarind concentrate, dissolved in 100 ml/scant ½ cup hot water
2 tablespoons soft brown sugar
3 tablespoons vegan fish sauce (page 13), light soy sauce or tamari
6 kaffir lime leaves
600 g/1 lb. 5 oz. smoked firm tofu, crumbled
vegetable oil, for deep-frying
4 garlic cloves, thinly sliced
1 banana shallot, thinly sliced
10 whole dried or fresh red bird's eye chillies/chiles, with stems
400 g/14 oz. kanom jin noodles
freshly squeezed juice of 4 limes
holy basil (optional), to garnish
Salsify & Chilli fritters (opposite) and fresh watercress with cucumber and chillies/chiles (optional), to serve

ROASTED PASTE

2 tablespoons mung beans, soaked in cold water for 1 hour and drained
4 garlic cloves, unpeeled
4 red shallots, or 2 small red onions, unpeeled
7.5-cm/3-in. piece of galangal or root ginger, peeled and cut into 2.5-cm/1-in. chunks
2 coriander/cilantro roots or a handful of fresh coriander/cilantro stems, chopped
a pinch of sea salt
½–1 tablespoon vegan fish sauce (page 13), or dark soy sauce
3–4 tablespoons Nam Prik Pao (page 101)

2 bamboo skewers, soaked in water

SERVES 4

To make the roasted paste, dry-fry the mung beans in a large frying pan/skillet until well toasted and nutty. Using a food processor, or a pestle and mortar, grind the mung beans to a powder.

Preheat the grill/broiler. Skewer the garlic cloves and shallots onto the soaked skewers and place on a baking sheet. Grill/broil until the skins starts to blacken. Leave to cool, then remove the blackened skins. Using a pestle and mortar, blend the roasted garlic and shallots with the mung bean powder, galangal, coriander/cilantro roots and salt. Alternatively, use a food processor or blender. Add just enough of the vegan fish sauce to help blend the ingredients to a smooth paste. Mix in the nam prik pao, then set aside.

Pour the coconut cream into a large pan, then add the roasted paste and bring gently to the boil, then reduce to a simmer. Add the tamarind liquid, sugar, vegan fish sauce and lime leaves. Add the crumbled tofu to the pan and simmer gently for a further 10–15 minutes.

Put 600 ml/generous 2½ cups vegetable oil in a large, heavy-based pan over medium-high heat. When hot, deep-fry the sliced garlic, the shallots and the bird's eye chillies/chiles in batches until dark brown and crispy. Lift out with a slotted spoon. Set aside.

Cook the noodles in boiling water and set aside. Check the seasoning for the tofu, then add the lime juice. The dish should taste as Thompson describes, "fragrantly sour, salty and sweet, yet slightly bitter and nutty". Place a portion of the noodles in each serving bowl, and spoon a generous amount of the tofu nahm prik over the top. Sprinkle with some of the deep-fried garlic, shallots and chillies/chiles and a sprig of holy basil, if you like. Serve with the suggested accompaniments, if you like.

SALSIFY & CHILLI FRITTERS

Thai vegetable fritters are a great vegan alternative to egg-based batters. You could use any vegetable really, but I think salsify – sometimes called an oyster plant – is a much under-rated vegetable. These fritters are incredibly moreish, and make a great topping for Kanom Jin Nahm Prik Tofu (opposite) or serve on their own with a dipping sauce.

2 salsify roots, peeled
1 teaspoon freshly squeezed lime juice
2 tablespoons cornflour/cornstarch
500 ml/2 cups vegetable oil, for deep-frying
3 large red and 3 large green chillies/chiles, halved lengthways and deseeded
dipping sauce of your choice, to serve (optional)

BATTER
2½ tablespoons rice flour
180 ml/¾ cup coconut milk, plus extra if needed
finely chopped zest and freshly squeezed juice of 1 unwaxed lime
1 teaspoon salt, or to taste

SERVES 2–4

Using a vegetable peeler, slice the salsify into thin strips lengthways. Put the strips in a bowl of cold water and add the teaspoon of lime juice to stop them browning.

To make the batter, whisk the rice flour with all the other ingredients in a bowl until smooth – it should have a pouring consistency; add a little more flour or coconut milk if required. Taste to check the seasoning and add more salt if needed. Put the cornflour/cornstarch on a plate.

Heat the vegetable oil in a large, heavy-based pan over medium-high heat. Test the oil with a little batter – it should sizzle and rise to the surface. Be careful not to overheat or the batter will burn.

Dip the salsify and chilli/chile lengths in the cornflour/cornstarch, then dip them into the batter mixture. In batches, gently lay the strips in the hot oil and fry until golden brown, turning occasionally. Set aside on paper towels to drain. Serve while hot.

KHAO SOI NOODLES
CHIANG MAI CURRY NOODLES

400 g/14 oz. egg-free
   yellow noodles
500 ml/2 cups vegetable
   oil, for deep-frying
8 small red chillies/chiles
1 small red onion, thinly
   sliced, to serve
60 g/2 oz. preserved
   mustard greens
   (optional), to serve
Nam Prik Pao (page 99),
   to serve
a handful of fresh
   coriander/cilantro,
   to serve
1 lime, cut into wedges,
   to serve
red chillies/chiles, baked
   whole until blackened,
   to serve

RED CURRY PASTE
1 tablespoon coriander
   seeds
1 teaspoon cumin seeds
1 teaspoon black
   peppercorns
4 garlic cloves, peeled
3 coriander/cilantro roots,
   or stems from ½ bunch
   of fresh coriander/
   cilantro, chopped
10–12 dried red chillies/
   chiles, chopped
2 lemongrass stalks,
   chopped
3 kaffir lime leaves
7.5-cm/3-in. piece of
   galangal, or root
   ginger, peeled and
   chopped
2 tablespoons vegan fish
   sauce (page 13)
vegetable oil, if needed

KHAO SOI PASTE
1 teaspoon coriander
   seeds
1 teaspoon black
   cardamom seeds
   from the pods
4 tablespoons ginger
   paste
1 tablespoon ground
   turmeric
1 teaspoon medium
   curry powder

BROTH
400 ml/1¾ cups coconut
   milk
500 ml/generous 2 cups
   vegetable stock
200 g/7 oz. canned green
   jackfruit (optional),
   washed, drained and
   chopped, or baked firm
   tofu or tofu puffs
100 g/1⅓ cups cauliflower
   florets
2 carrots, sliced
   diagonally
150 g/5 oz. mangetouts/
   snow peas
1 sweet potato, chopped
   into 2-cm/¾-in. cubes
1 tablespoon soft brown
   sugar
1 tablespoon light soy
   sauce
1 tablespoon dark soy
   sauce
sea salt, if needed

SERVES 4–6

To make the red curry paste, toast the coriander and cumin seeds in a dry pan over medium heat for 30 seconds, stirring occasionally, to release the aroma. Finely grind the seeds and peppercorns to a powder in a spice grinder or using a pestle and mortar. Put all the remaining ingredients in a food processor or blender and add the toasted spices, then blend to a smooth paste, adding a little oil if necessary. Store in a glass jar for up to 1 month.

For the khao soi paste, toast the coriander seeds and black cardamom seeds in a dry pan over medium heat for 30 seconds, stirring occasionally, then finely grind them to a powder in a spice grinder or using a pestle and mortar. Put 4 tablespoons of the red curry paste in a bowl and mix in the ground spices and the remaining khao soi paste ingredients.

Cook 300 g/11 oz. of the noodles according to the pack instructions, then drain and set aside. Put the vegetable oil in a heavy-based pan and heat over a medium-high heat, then add the remaining noodles and fry them until crispy and puffed up. Set aside on paper towels to drain.

Preheat the oven to 200°C (400°F) Gas 6.

Place the chillies/chiles on a baking sheet and bake in the preheated oven for 10–12 minutes, until starting to blacken. Set aside to cool.

To make the broth, put the khao soi paste in a large, heavy-based pan and add the coconut milk, stock and 500 ml/generous 2 cups water. Bring to the boil, then reduce to a simmer. Add the jackfruit, if using. Cook gently for 15 minutes, then add the remaining vegetables, sugar and soy sauces, and cook for a further 10 minutes. Check the seasoning and add more salt or vegan fish sauce if needed.

To serve, place the boiled noodles in serving bowls, then add some broth. Top with some fried noodles, sliced red onion, mustard greens (if using), a small spoonful of nam prik pao and some fresh coriander/cilantro leaves. Serve with lime wedges and whole baked chillies/chiles.

This crowd-pleasing dish hails from Chiang Mai, the ancient capital of the northern province and one of the oldest cities in Thailand. Packed with beautiful temples and great food that reflects the diversity of influences and its proximity to the ancient silk routes. We passed through this modern, busy city on our month-long journey along the border with Burma, through Mae Sot and Mae Hong Son. Planning to hop on a boat and follow the Mekong into Laos, we heard horror stories of sitting on a plastic chair for 16 hours on an overfilled boat in a dry, pre-monsoon river. This sounded highly unappealing with two seven-year-olds, so we opted for the one flight a day to Luang Prabang, meaning we had to wait a few days to get seats.

GLASS NOODLES WITH CASHEW & CHILLI

This recipe is based on the very first dish I ate in Thailand. We were on a train from Bangkok to Butterworth, an overnight journey, and Lee and I were completely unprepared. We sat in our assigned seats (or so we thought), and while we were admiring the spaciousness and cleanliness of our second-class air-con carriage, Lee discovered a small plastic bag of something smelly. Thinking it was rubbish he proceeded to remove it, and dropped it in the bin on the platform. After settling back down, an elderly Thai couple arrived and, after much gesticulation, we understood that we were in their seats, and the elderly lady was repeatedly asking 'Where see baa?' It then became rapidly clear that whatever we had thrown away belonged to them! It turned out to be their dinner of sea bass, which Lee then fished out of the bin (fortunately unscathed) and returned to them with profuse and embarrassed apologies.

As the train left the station, we realised that most of our fellow passengers had brought their own food and drinks for the journey and we were going to have to rely on the train menu (wholly in Thai). The only Thai word I knew at this point was jay (vegetarian) and we ended up being served glass noodles with lots of tiny and mind-blowingly hot chillies/chiles. This recipe is obviously a tempered-down version. It can be served hot, or cold as a salad. I sometimes serve this dish with Thai Sweetcorn & Spring Onion Patties (page 114) for a fragrant Thai dinner.

6–12 dried bird's eye chillies/chiles
150 g/5 oz. glass (cellophane) noodles
100 g/heaped ¾ cup cashew nuts
1 tablespoon vegetable oil
2 tablespoons soft brown sugar
1 tablespoon soy sauce
2 tablespoons vegan fish sauce (page 13)
8 spring onions/scallions, sliced
2 tomatoes, chopped
2 limes, cut in half
sea salt and ground white pepper
fresh coriander/cilantro leaves, to garnish

SERVES 2–4

Put the dried chillies/chiles in a bowl and cover with hot water, then leave to soak. Drain and set aside. Break up the noodles into a pan of boiling water over high heat and cook for 4–5 minutes, then drain and plunge them into a bowl of cold water. Drain in a colander and set aside.

Toast the cashews in a dry pan over medium heat for 1–2 minutes, stirring occasionally, until golden. Set aside in a bowl.

In the same pan, add the oil, then add the sugar, soy sauce, vegan fish sauce and the soaked chillies/chiles. Cook over high heat for 2 minutes, then add the noodles and toss well to coat with the dressing.

Add half the cashews, the spring onions/scallions and tomato, and cook for 2 minutes. Add a couple of pinches of salt and mix well.

Serve immediately, topped with the remaining nuts, a squeeze of lime and a sprinkle of fresh coriander/cilantro and white pepper.

GAENG KEOW WAN
TRADITIONAL THAI GREEN CURRY

There are numerous sources for recipes for Thai green curry. I've included this one here because I think it's a fairly authentic and super-easy version to make, and it's always a crowd-pleaser, both at the family dinner table and in a field full of festival goers. The paste will keep for at least 1 month in the fridge. Roasting some of the vegetables adds some depth of flavour and means that the sauce can be cooked for a shorter time, so it maintains the fresh taste of the herbs and prevents the coconut milk from splitting. You can add baked tofu or tofu puffs to this recipe for extra protein and texture.

½ butternut squash, peeled, deseeded and cut into bite-sized pieces
1 aubergine/eggplant, cut into bite-sized pieces
2 carrots, thinly sliced diagonally
100 g/3¾ oz. green beans, trimmed
120 g/1½ cups cauliflower florets
400 ml/1¾ cups coconut milk
½ teaspoon salt, or to taste
2 tablespoons light soy sauce
1 litre/4⅓ cups vegetable stock
steamed jasmine rice, to serve

GREEN CURRY PASTE
2 teaspoons ground coriander
2 teaspoons ground cumin
2 teaspoons freshly ground black pepper
8 green jalapeño chillies/chiles, trimmed
8 green bird's eye chillies/chiles, trimmed
2 small red onions, chopped
6 garlic cloves, chopped
5-cm/2-in. piece of galangal or root ginger, peeled and chopped
4 lemongrass stalks, chopped
8 kaffir lime leaves
½ bunch of fresh coriander/cilantro, including stems
a bunch of Thai basil, including stems

2 baking sheets, generously greased

SERVES 4–5

To make the green curry paste, toast the ground coriander and cumin in a dry pan over medium heat for 30 seconds, stirring occasionally, to release the aroma, and then add the ground black pepper. Put the spices and all the remaining ingredients in a food processor or blender and blend together until smooth. Alternatively, use a pestle and mortar, which is more authentic but rather time-consuming.

Preheat the oven to 220°C (425°F) Gas 7.

Put the squash and aubergine/eggplant on the prepared baking sheets, and season with salt. Roast for about 15–20 minutes, or until soft and the edges are browned.

To make the curry, add 1 generous tablespoon green curry paste per person to a large pan and fry gently for 5 minutes. Add the prepared vegetables (including the roast squash and aubergine/eggplant), the coconut milk, salt, soy sauce and vegetable stock. Stir and bring to the boil. Simmer for 7–8 minutes. Check the seasoning and add more salt if needed. Serve with steamed jasmine rice.

MARMALADE TOFU WITH CHILLI & CASHEWS

Thai oranges are sweeter and less acidic than their European counterparts, and there's really nothing quite like the freshly squeezed juice that's readily available from street vendors everywhere. We first came across a version of this dish, based on Thai orange chicken, in a little café called Cha Chai in Koh Phayam, a relatively undeveloped island in the Andaman Sea. My recipe is easy and quick to make, so perfect for a mid-week dinner. You can use a vegan chicken substitute instead of tofu, and I recommend using a good-quality marmalade.

60 g/½ cup cashew nuts (whole or broken)
8–16 dried chillies (the fat, red variety, to taste), soaked in boiling water for 30 minutes, then drained
2 tablespoons vegetable oil
400 g/14 oz. firm tofu or vegan chicken substitute, cut into 1–2-cm/½–1-in. cubes
2 large garlic cloves, chopped
1 tablespoon finely chopped root ginger or ginger paste
2–3 tablespoons good-quality marmalade
2 tablespoons light soy sauce
steamed rice, to serve

SERVES 4

Toast the nuts in a dry frying pan/skillet or wok for 4–5 minutes, tossing them gently, until they start to brown, then set aside.

Roughly tear the soaked chillies/chiles. The seeds can easily be separated at this stage, so only keep a few seeds so the dish is not too spicy but has lots of flavour. Set aside.

Add 1 tablespoon vegetable oil to the pan and fry the tofu pieces over medium heat in the pan until brown and starting to crisp on all sides, then set aside. (Alternatively, preheat the oven to 190°C (375°F) Gas 5, place the tofu pieces on a well oiled baking sheet and bake for 10–15 minutes. I prefer this method as it produces a crispier texture.)

Add the remaining vegetable oil to the pan, add the garlic and ginger and fry gently for about 5–7 minutes until golden brown. Add the tofu, nuts, chillies/chiles, marmalade, soy sauce and 4 tablespoons water.

Bring to a simmer and cook for 2–3 minutes more. Add a little more water if the dish gets too dry, and to create more sauce. Serve immediately with steamed rice.

SWEETCORN & SPRING ONION PATTIES

These delicious little fritters are known locally as tod man khao pod. If you have made a stock of Thai green curry paste, they are also super-quick to prepare. I serve them on my street food menu with Peanut & Cucumber Dipping Sauce (opposite).

350 g/2½ cups
    sweetcorn/corn
    kernels, canned
    or frozen
4 spring onions/scallions,
    thinly sliced
2–3 tablespoons green
    curry paste (page 112)
2 tablespoons plain/
    all-purpose flour

2 tablespoons rice flour
2 tablespoons vegan fish
    sauce (page 13),
    or light soy sauce
    or tamari
1–2 teaspoons salt
vegetable oil, for
    deep-frying

MAKES 16–20

Put half the sweetcorn/corn and spring onions/scallions in a food processor or blender with all the remaining ingredients, except the salt and oil, and process until the sweetcorn is roughly broken up and well mixed with the other ingredients. Pour the batter into a bowl and mix in the remaining sweetcorn/corn and spring onions/scallions. Season with salt to taste.

Preheat the oven to 110°C (225°F) Gas ¼ and put a baking sheet in to warm. Heat the oil in a wok or large, heavy-based pan to 180°C (350°F). Test the oil with a little batter mix, to ensure that it sizzles. Using a dessertspoon, gently drop spoonfuls of the batter into the hot oil and deep-fry, in batches, for 5–8 minutes until golden brown and cooked through. Drain on paper towels. Keep the cooked patties warm on the baking sheet in the oven while you cook the remaining batches. (Alternatively, you can reheat them later in a moderate oven for 10 minutes.) Serve hot.

PEANUT & CUCUMBER DIPPING SAUCE

Thai street food is served with a variety of sauces on the side, where skewers and fried snacks are often accompanied by a sweet and spicy sauce. I serve this quick and versatile sauce with the patties opposite and Sticky BBQ Tofu Skewers (page 102).

¼ cucumber, peeled and
    halved lengthways
1 teaspoon light soy
    sauce
3 tablespoons freshly
    squeezed lime juice
2–3 teaspoons soft brown
    sugar, to taste
1 tablespoon peanuts
2 tablespoons rice
    vinegar

1 red shallot or ½ small
    red onion, finely
    chopped
1 green chilli/chile,
    finely chopped
1 red chilli/chile,
    finely chopped
a pinch of salt

SERVES 4

Using a teaspoon, scrape out the watery seeds from the centre of the cucumber, then slice the flesh thinly into crescents.

Put the soy sauce in a bowl and add the lime juice and sugar. Stir together until dissolved.

Dry-roast the peanuts in small frying pan/skillet over medium heat for 4–5 minutes, stirring occasionally, until starting to brown. Leave to cool.

Using a pestle and mortar, grind or crush the peanuts to a rough, chunky powder.

Add this peanut powder and all the remaining ingredients to the soy sauce mixture and stir well before pouring over the prepared cucumber and tossing to coat in the dressing.

SOM TAM RICE PAPER ROLLS
THAI GREEN PAPAYA SALAD ROLLS

I made this dish for the critic's menu during MasterChef 2011. Although both John and Gregg liked the dish, I followed a very authentic approach and created something that was far too spicy for the average Western palate, giving both Gregg and Tracey MacLeod, a much-respected food critic, the infamous chilli/chile hiccups. It's up to you to adjust the amount of chilli/chile you want to use. I like it super-hot, and it balances against the sweet and salty flavours, but use fewer chillies/chiles if you want something with less heat.

150 g/heaped 1 cup unsalted peanuts

2–8 red bird's-eye chillies/chiles, to taste, thinly sliced

6 garlic cloves, peeled and left whole

1 green papaya, peeled, deseeded and grated

1 small carrot, grated

a large handful of green beans, trimmed and cut into 2.5-cm/1-in. pieces

10 cherry tomatoes, quartered

3 tablespoons vegan fish sauce (page 13), or vegetarian Worcestershire sauce, or light soy sauce

3 tablespoons light soy sauce

freshly squeezed juice of 2 limes

3 tablespoons grated palm sugar/jaggery

12 sheets of Vietnamese rice paper

a handful of fresh coriander/cilantro or basil leaves and/or edible flowers (optional), to garnish

SERVES 4

Preheat the oven to 200°C (400°F) Gas 6.

Scatter the peanuts onto a baking sheet and put in the preheated oven for 8–10 minutes until the peanuts are golden brown and well roasted. Set aside.

Put the chillies/chiles and garlic in a large mortar and grind with a pestle to make a paste. Set the paste aside in a small bowl.

Put the papaya, carrot and green beans in the mortar, and pound gently. Add the cherry tomatoes and pound again for a few minutes until well bruised. Add the vegan fish sauce, soy sauce, lime juice and sugar, and continue to pound until all the ingredients are well mixed. Stir in the chilli/chile and garlic paste.

Set up a large bowl of hot water next to the chopping board. Soak each rice paper sheet for 2–3 minutes in hot water or according to the packet instructions just prior to filling and rolling as follows. Soak the paper until soft, then lay it on a clean dish towel and pat it dry with paper towels. Put it onto the chopping board and put about a twelfth of the papaya mixture in the centre, leaving a 3-cm/1¼-in border all the way round. Fold in the sides, then roll the paper tightly to create a cigar shape. Repeat with the remaining sheets of rice paper and papaya mixture. Slice the rolls in half at an angle. Serve six pieces per person. Garnish with the herbs or edible flowers, if you like.

MUNG BEAN VEGETABLE NOODLE SOUP

It's hard to turn a corner in Thailand without seeing a noodle soup vendor, and it soon becomes a staple dish in any traveller's diet. The traditional vegetable noodle soup uses mung bean or thread noodles (sometimes called glass or cellophane noodles), but you could substitute any rice noodles. You can make the soup more substantial by adding Ginger Baked Tofu (page 198) as a topping at the end, but I like the simplicity of this dish that makes for a quick and filling lunch.

375 g/13 oz. mung bean noodles or rice vermicelli noodles
1 tablespoon toasted sesame oil
1 tablespoon vegetable oil
8 garlic cloves, crushed
1 tablespoon finely chopped galangal, or fresh root ginger
2 litres/quarts vegetable stock or water

2 tablespoons vegan fish sauce (page 13), or soy sauce or tamari
3 tablespoons light soy sauce, or tamari
1 teaspoon soft brown sugar
1 stick of lemongrass, bruised with a rolling pin
100 g/3½ oz. shredded white cabbage
100 g/3½ oz. shredded dark green cabbage or kale
1 carrot, coarsely grated or cut into julienne
120 g/2 cups beansprouts
4 spring onions/scallions, sliced (including the green parts)
freshly squeezed juice of 1 lime
2 red chillies/chiles, finely sliced, to garnish

SERVES 3–4

Put the noodles in a large bowl and cover with boiling water. Leave for 4–5 minutes until the noodles are soft. Rinse, drain and set aside.

Heat the sesame and vegetable oils in a large pan over medium heat and cook the garlic and galangal for 3–4 minutes, until golden brown and starting to crisp. (At this stage, I sometimes put the crispy fried garlic and galangal back into a mortar, bash them a little to make a rough paste, then return to the pan.) Add the vegetable stock and bring to the boil. Add the vegan fish sauce, soy sauce, sugar and bruised lemongrass. Bring to the boil, then simmer for 5 minutes.

Add the shredded cabbages, carrot, beansprouts, three-quarters of the chopped spring onions/scallions and the noodles, then return to the boil and immediately remove from the heat. Remove the lemongrass and add the lime juice.

To serve, pour into large, deep bowls and top each bowl with the remaining spring onions/scallions and sliced chillies/chiles.

BANANA & PINEAPPLE FRITTERS WITH ORANGE BLOSSOM CARAMEL

Deep-fried fruit is a common snack in South-east Asia, with lots of variations of batters. I served a variation of this dish on my summer street food menu during 2013, and it gave the Rhubarb Samosas (page 72) a run for their money. The crispy coconut batter is naturally gluten-free, and if you don't fancy making caramel, just add a drizzle of golden/light corn syrup or maple syrup instead.

1 small pineapple, peeled, cored and sliced into rings
6 bananas, peeled and cut in half lengthways

CARAMEL
1 tablespoon liquid glucose, or a pinch of cream of tartar
200 g/1 cup unrefined sugar
300 ml/generous 1¼ cups coconut milk, at room temperature
2–3 teaspoons orange blossom water

BATTER
125 g/1 cup rice flour
4 tablespoons cassava/tapioca flour
2 tablespoons caster/superfine sugar
½ teaspoon salt
50 g/⅔ cup desiccated/dry unsweetened shredded coconut
500 ml/2 cups vegetable oil, for deep-frying

SERVES 4–6

To make the caramel, put 60 ml/¼ cup water in a heavy-based pan and add the glucose and sugar. Stir the mixture to help dissolve the sugar, then gently bring to a simmer over medium heat, without stirring. The key to making a good caramel is avoiding the formation of sugar crystals. The glucose or cream of tartar helps to prevent this. It is also important not to stir the mixture once it is heating. Swirl the pan to encourage the sugar to dissolve. Heat until the mixture is clear, then turn up the heat slightly and simmer until it becomes deep brown (but not burnt). This can take 10–15 minutes. Remove from the heat, then carefully whisk in the coconut milk. It will bubble and splutter, so take care. Add the orange blossom water and stir well. The caramel can be stored in a glass bottle in the fridge for 1 month.

To make the batter, put the flours in a large bowl and add the sugar, salt and coconut. Stir in 300 ml/generous 1¼ cups water to make a thick batter.

Gently reheat the caramel sauce in a small pan over a medium-low heat until warm, if prepared in advance. Preheat the oven to 110°C (225°F) Gas ¼ and put a baking sheet in to warm. Heat the oil for deep-frying in a wok or a large, heavy-based pan over medium heat. Test the oil with a little batter mix, to ensure that it sizzles.

Cooking in batches, dip the prepared pineapple and banana pieces in the batter, ensuring that they are well coated, and then gently lay them in the hot oil. Fry until golden brown. Drain on paper towels. Keep the fritters warm on the baking sheet while you cook the remaining batches. Serve the hot-and-crispy fruit pieces drizzled with the caramel sauce.

KHAAW NEOW MA MUANG
STICKY COCONUT RICE WITH MANGO

For me, tuk-tuks – the three-wheeled motorized taxis – feel like putting your life in the hands of someone who believes he will be reincarnated. I found this quite alarming at first, as my lack of belief in an afterlife or second life meant I was quite keen to stay in this one. The kids on the other hand would choose the rollercoaster ride that is the tuk-tuk over any other way of getting around Bangkok. Once my worst fears started to abate, I began to enjoy how close you feel to the street in a tuk-tuk – a bit like being on a bicycle, only much faster.

It was while zipping along the Ratchadamnoen Klang road that our tuk-tuk driver took a shortcut, and as we bumped our way down a side street, or soi, we came across a sticky-rice-and-mango seller. This dish was so good. I challenge anyone who's eaten it not to remember exactly when they first tried it. I was in awe of how such simple ingredients could combine to make something that tasted like food of the gods. Thailand's answer to salted caramel puddings.

The best mango to use is the golden-skinned, slightly pointy Asian mango rather than the round red-orange mangoes from the West Indies. Mango season starts around April, so that's the best time to get the tastiest ones, but they are generally available until September. Bananas make a good substitute if you can't get hold of mangoes, or if they're a little expensive. Using glutinous rice is essential.

100 g/½ cup Thai glutinous rice, soaked in water for at least 1 hour
400 ml/1¾ cups coconut milk with a high percentage of coconut
1½ tablespoons sugar
¼ teaspoon salt
1 sweet, ripe yellow mango, halved, stoned/pitted and peeled

1–2 pinches of black sesame seeds
fresh mint leaves, to garnish

SAUCE
a large pinch of salt
1½ teaspoons sugar
½ teaspoon cornflour/cornstarch

SERVES 2

Steam the rice according to the packet instructions or following the advice on page 13.

Do not shake the can of coconut. Remove the creamiest part, put it into a small bowl and set aside. Pour the liquid into a pan and set over medium heat. Add the sugar and salt, then stir to dissolve. Mix this liquid through the cooked sticky rice. It will appear quite loose, but stir in well, then cover with a clean dish towel and set aside. The rice will absorb the liquid. Cool to room temperature – do not chill.

To make the sauce, put the reserved coconut cream in a small pan and add a generous pinch of salt and the sugar. Heat gently until dissolved. Mix the cornflour/cornstarch with 2 tablespoons cold water, stir it into the mixture and continue to stir over low heat until it becomes thick and creamy. Taste and adjust to taste with more salt and sugar.

Cut each mango half into 6 slices. Spoon some rice onto each serving plate, then lay 6 mango pieces on the plate. Pour some of the sauce onto the mango and rice, then scatter with sesame seeds and garnish with mint leaves just before serving.

Laos

The people of Laos were some of the most contented people I had ever met on this planet. Probably a reflection of being cut off from the rest of the world (and tourism) for so many years. Our experience of Laos was as a very beautiful and gentle place. Old bomb shells from the Vietnam war make for all manner of herb pots, planters and fencing material in villages. It is far from being a wealthy country, but the fertile land allows people to produce plenty on their tiny plots. They have a penchant for pig lungs and chicken feet, but they also understand vegetarianism (unlike Vietnam, where it's hard to find a soup or sauce without a bone-based broth).

We ate some of the best noodle soups in Laos, which seemed heavily influenced by those in north-eastern Thailand with fearsome levels of chilli/chile heat and vegetables I couldn't name. Of course, there are the French influences as well, commonly found across Cambodia and Vietnam, too. So strictly speaking, I can't even say these dishes are solely Laotian, or Vietnamese, inspired. It's just about what we ate while we travelled, and what I wanted to adapt and cook when I returned home.

We travelled across Laos with the intention of exploring Vietnam, but found ourselves overwhelmed by the pre-monsoon heat and so once we had enjoyed the saturated fun of the water festival Pii Mai Laos, we decided to make a u-turn and head south again. One day, I plan to return to Laos and Vietnam as I have much more exploring (and eating) to do. But not in April next time!

MUANG NGOI, NORTHERN LAOS We spent several weeks staying in small villages as we travelled through Northern Laos, and the children made many new local friends. Roisin became inseparable from her new friend Marika, and the children were often invited for dinner or even to take part in village rituals and ceremonies. They probably enjoyed some of their happiest travelling days in those northern hills (apart from the extraordinary and incessant humidity).

I originally wanted the first recipe in this section to be Marika's mum's Mekong wafers. Malychanh made these delicious crispy, savoury and salty dark green wafers from Mekong river algae, which is cleaned, dried and flattened. It's then thinly smattered with a concoction of sesame seeds, garlic, tomato, galangal and onion, and dried in the sunshine. I had no idea what they were called and had seen a glimpse of how potentially difficult they would be to try and make (starting with the fact that fresh Mekong river algae is unlikely to be in the fridge in Chinatown). Then I was reading the marvellous Ant Egg Soup, tales of a food tourist in Laos, and there it was. A little sketch of kai pen which looked just like Malychanh's algae gathering. Kai pen remains impossible for me to recreate but if you ever get to Laos, I highly recommend trying some.

From left to right: Village children, Northern Laos; Monks in Luang Prabang; Nam Ou River, Laos; Laos fisherman; Mountain range between Vang Vieng and Luang Prabang; Local girl in northern Laos; Temple nagas, Wat Tham Phou Si, Luang Prabang.

LAOS-STYLE ROASTED PUMPKIN, COCONUT & CHILLI SOUP

Sweet vegetables and spicy chilli/chile make for a delicious flavour balance in this super simple recipe, so you could substitute the pumpkin for sweet potato or even parsnip, if you like. Roasting the vegetables creates a much more intense flavour in this creamy silky soup. I like to serve it with big hunks of crusty bread.

2 tablespoons vegetable oil
1 small pumpkin or butternut squash, peeled, deseeded and cubed
2–4 large red chillies/chiles, to taste, trimmed
1 litre/4⅓ cups vegetable stock
800 ml/3½ cups coconut milk
2 teaspoons salt, or to taste
2–3 tablespoons almond cream, or any vegan cream such as soya/soy or coconut cream

SERVES 4–6

Preheat the oven to 220°C (425°F) Gas 7.

Drizzle the oil onto a baking sheet. Put the pumpkin on the baking sheet and toss to coat in the oil. Roast for 20–30 minutes until it begins to brown and soften. Put the chillies/chiles on the baking sheet for the last 8–10 minutes and roast until they begin to blacken.

Put the stock in a large pan and add 1 litre/4⅓ cups water and the roasted vegetables. Bring to the boil, then reduce to a simmer and add the coconut milk. Return to the boil, then simmer gently for 10 minutes. Using a food processor or stick blender, blend the soup until smooth and creamy. Season with the salt to taste.

Divide the soup into serving bowls and finish each with a swirl of almond cream.

LEMONGRASS SOUP WITH WONTONS

This substantial soup makes a refreshing change from noodles. Lemongrass is very popular in Laos, probably because it grows everywhere, and it is often used to flavour ceviche or baked river fish, as well as soups. I love dumplings in soup, and the great thing about any kind of dumpling is that it can easily be adapted to a vegan diet. Wontons tend to come with quite meaty fillings, so I use firm tofu and dried mushrooms. I buy my wonton wrappers from the Chinese supermarket, but always check the ingredients, as some are made with egg.

3 lemongrass stalks, finely chopped

1 tablespoon vegetable oil

1 litre/4¼ cups vegetable stock

3 tablespoons freshly squeezed lime juice

1 tablespoon vegan fish sauce (page 13), or 1 tablespoon light soy sauce and a pinch of dried seaweed

3 kaffir lime leaves

½ red chilli/chile, thinly sliced

½ green chilli/chile, thinly sliced

1 teaspoon soft brown sugar

a handful of fresh coriander/cilantro leaves, chopped, to garnish

a handful of holy basil leaves, or a mixture of mint and European basil leaves, to garnish

1 lime, quartered and then halved, for squeezing

DUMPLINGS

80 g/3⅓ cups dried Chinese mushrooms or other dried mushrooms

1 teaspoon sesame oil

1 small red onion, finely chopped

5-cm/2-in. piece of galangal or root ginger, peeled and finely chopped

140 g/5 oz. firm tofu, crumbled

100 g/¾ cup water chestnuts, chopped

½–1 tablespoon dark soy sauce

12 egg-free wonton wrappers

plain/all-purpose, to dust

vegetable oil, for deep-frying (optional)

salt

SERVES 3–4

To make the dumplings, soak the mushrooms in boiling water for 10–15 minutes, then drain and finely chop. Put the sesame oil in a small frying pan/skillet over medium heat and cook the onion for 5 minutes or until softened. Add the galangal and mushrooms. Cook for 10 minutes or until the liquid is reduced, then add all the remaining ingredients, except the wonton wrappers, and stir well. Remove from the heat and season with salt. Set aside to cool slightly.

Pound the lemongrass in a mortar using a pestle to make a rough pulp. Heat the vegetable oil in a deep pan or wok over medium heat, then add the lemongrass pulp and gently stir-fry for 5 minutes. Add all the remaining ingredients, bring to the boil and simmer gently for 10 minutes.

Put a wonton wrapper on a lightly floured surface, then put 1 teaspoon of the mushroom filling in the centre. Lightly brush the edges of the pastry with water, then pinch the opposite corners together. To seal, twist the corners slightly. Repeat to make 12 dumplings.

When all the dumplings are prepared, gently put them all into the simmering broth to cook. As soon as the dumplings float – about 5 minutes – remove the pan from the heat. To server, place 3–4 cooked wontons in each serving bowl, ladle the broth over the top, garnish with herbs and add a squeeze of lime juice. (Alternatively, you can deep-fry the wontons to produce a crispy dumpling as shown opposite and serve them alongside the broth.)

From left to right: Vegetable Laap with
Sticky Rice; Aubergine Jeow.

VEGETABLE LAAP WITH STICKY RICE
LAOS-STYLE WARM SALAD WITH VEGETABLES

It seemed like there were chickens everywhere in Laos. On the bus, on your lap, under the table, on the balcony at 4.00am. When the animals wake up in Laos, it's time for you to wake up. And chicken is on the menu a lot. In one village, they referred to chicken-based dishes as 'suzi'. We were never entirely sure whether suzi was the actual chicken or not. Laotians have a penchant for eating this dish raw (laap dip) with either minced chicken or pork, and it often contains some kind of innard or entrail, as did many freshly cooked dishes. This could sometimes make it a challenge to find good vegetarian food (and not the piles of less-than-fresh cold salads you see in Luang Prabang). We ate a lot of noodle soups and banana pancakes in Laos! On returning home, I was keen to make my own vegan laap, which is equally delicious, as the oyster mushrooms provide a great meaty texture to go with all the fragrant flavours.

380 g/2 cups glutinous
    rice
½ teaspoon salt
1 tablespoon vegetable
    oil
120 g/4 oz. oyster
    mushrooms, roughly
    torn and chopped
120 g/4 oz. brown shimeji
    mushrooms, or
    chestnut/cremini
    mushrooms
1 red (bell) pepper,
    deseeded and
    chopped into 1-cm/
    ½-in. pieces
4 garlic cloves, chopped
2 teaspoons soy sauce,
    or tamari
2–3 teaspoons cornflour/
    cornstarch
1 Little Gem/Bibb lettuce,
    leaves separated and
    rinsed

1 small red onion, finely
    sliced
a small handful of fresh
    Thai basil, mint and
    coriander/cilantro
    leaves, roughly torn
2 small red chillies/chiles,
    finely sliced

SAUCE
2 tablespoons vegan fish
    sauce (page 13), or
    light soy sauce or
    tamari
1 tablespoon soy sauce
1–2 teaspoons soft brown
    sugar
2 small red chillies/chiles,
    finely chopped
freshly squeezed juice
    of 2 limes

SERVES 2–3

To make the sticky rice, soak the glutinous rice in a bowl of cold water for 1–2 hours or even overnight. Drain well.

Put the rice in a pan with 840 ml/3½ cups water and the salt. Bring to the boil and simmer with the lid half-off for 10 minutes, then turn off the heat and place the lid on fully. Leave to stand for 10 minutes, then fluff up the rice with a fork to check it is evenly cooked. Alternatively use an electric rice steamer or a traditional bamboo basket. Place the basket in a colander over a large pan of boiling water, and cover.

Meanwhile, mix together the sauce ingredients and stir well to make sure the sugar has dissolved. Set aside.

Heat the vegetable oil in a frying pan/skillet over high heat. Place the mushrooms, red (bell) pepper and garlic in a bowl with the soy sauce and 2 teaspoons of the cornflour/cornstarch. Mix well and add the remaining cornflour/cornstarch if necessary, then immediately add to the hot pan. Fry over high heat for about 8–10 minutes until crispy and golden brown all over.

Fill the lettuce leaves with the vegetable mixture and drizzle over the sauce. Sprinkle some sliced red onion, herbs and fresh chillies/chiles over the top. Serve immediately with the sticky rice and any remaining sauce.

AUBERGINE JEOW

SPICY AUBERGINE/EGGPLANT DIP

Laos food often involves roasting skewered chillies/chiles, shallots and other vegetables on a hot barbecue. Jeow refers to the roasted chilli/chile sauce, served alongside other dishes, and it's sometimes made into a dip using aubergines or tomatoes. It's important to use a pestle and mortar for this recipe, or failing that a fork. A blender is too harsh on the texture, and affects the authentic flavour of the dish too. I like to serve this with some simple sticky rice for a light snack, or alongside some laap for a vegan Laos-style dinner.

2 medium-large
    aubergines/eggplants
    or 4 long thin ones
8 fat garlic cloves, skin on
6–10 small red chillies/
    chiles, to taste
2 banana shallots, skin on
freshly squeezed juice of
    1 lime
1–2 tablespoons vegan
    fish sauce (page 13),
    or light soy sauce
a handful of fresh
    coriander/cilantro,
    roughly chopped
a sprig or two of fresh
    mint, to garnish
    (optional)
salt, to taste

STICKY RICE
380 g/2 cups glutinous
    rice
½ teaspoon salt

4–6 bamboo skewers

SERVES 3–4

To make the sticky rice, soak the glutinous rice in a bowl of cold water for 1–2 hours or even overnight. Drain well.

Put the rice in a pan with 840 ml/3½ cups water and the salt. Bring to the boil and simmer with the lid half-off for 10 minutes, then turn off the heat and place the lid on fully. Leave to stand for 10 minutes, then fluff up the rice with a fork to check it is evenly cooked. Alternatively, use an electric rice steamer or a traditional bamboo basket. Place the basket in a colander over a large pan of boiling water, and cover.

Preheat the oven to 220°C (425°F) Gas 7.

To make the jeow, place the aubergines on a baking sheet, and bake in the preheated oven for about 30 minutes until the skins are starting to blacken. Set aside to cool.

Slide the garlic cloves, chillies/chiles and shallots onto the bamboo skewers and roast in the same way until they are also starting to blacken on the outside. They will cook at different times, so make sure you remove the garlic and chillies/chiles before they burn.

Once all the vegetables have cooled, remove the tops and skins from each, apart from the chillies, which only need the tops removing.

Set aside two of the roasted chillies/chiles, and then pound all the other cooked vegetables together using a pestle and mortar until it reaches a pulpy consistency. Add the lime juice and 1–2 tablespoons of the vegan fish sauce. Adjust the seasoning to taste, adding more salt if necessary.

Add the fresh coriander/cilantro and mix well. Serve in a large bowl, garnish with the reserved roasted chillies/chiles and a few sprigs of fresh mint (if using).

Serve the sticky rice in a bamboo rice basket, or a bowl. Alternatively, you can make sticky rice balls, for dipping into the jeow.

SIAM SOUP
FRAGRANT VEGETABLE NOODLE SOUP

Noodle soup is everywhere in South-east Asia, and especially in Thailand and Laos. The little roadside stalls set up a few plastic chairs and tables alongside their wok and cart, and, hey presto, you have an al fresco noodle-soup café. Unlike many other street foods, this one requires the diner to take a seat in order to eat. I have spent many hours sitting in my little plastic chair, slurping my soup and watching the world go by. This recipe is based on the one we all loved to eat while sitting alongside the banks of the Mekong River in the very pretty Luang Prabang in Laos. In our favourite riverside haunt, with its weird, giant glass jar of deceased creatures, the children updated their travel journals while Lee and I enjoyed a cheeky Beer Laos.

300 g/11 oz. dried, flat rice noodles, 5 mm–1 cm/¼–½ in. wide

400 g/14 oz. firm tofu, rinsed, drained and cut into bite-sized pieces, or you can use tofu puffs and omit the baking

6 garlic cloves, thinly sliced

7.5-cm/3-in. piece of root ginger, peeled and thinly sliced, then diced to make small cubes

2 small carrots, sliced diagonally

1 small courgette/zucchini, sliced diagonally

½ small cauliflower, cut into small florets

120 g/4 oz. green beans, cut into 2.5-cm/1-in. pieces

1 litre/4 cups vegetable stock

2–3 lemongrass stalks, to taste, bruised

6 kaffir lime leaves

800 ml/3½ cups coconut milk, or 1 block of creamed coconut, roughly chopped

6 tablespoons light soy sauce or tamari

4 tablespoons vegan fish sauce (page 13), or vegetarian Worcestershire sauce

salt, to taste

8 vegan 'scallop balls' or 'prawns/shrimp' (optional)

2 large red chillies/chiles, sliced (optional)

150 g/2¾ cups beansprouts

a small handful of fresh coriander/cilantro leaves

2 large red chillies/chiles or pickled chillies/chiles, sliced, to serve

1 lime, halved

baking sheet, greased

SERVES 4–6

Preheat the oven to 190°C (375°F) Gas 5.

Put the noodles in a large bowl. Add hand-hot water to cover. Soak for 5–10 minutes until soft but with plenty of bite. Rinse, drain and set aside.

Put the tofu on the prepared baking sheet. Bake for 10–15 minutes or until starting to crisp and turn golden brown. (Alternatively, you can fry the tofu in 2–3 tablespoons oil, then drain on paper towels.)

Heat the oil in a large pan over medium heat and add the garlic and ginger. Cook for 3–4 minutes or until they start to turn golden. Add the vegetables to the pan and cook for 2–3 minutes, then add the vegetable stock and 1 litre/4⅓ cups boiling water.

Add the lemongrass and lime leaves, then add the coconut milk, soy sauce and vegan fish sauce. If using creamed coconut, add 500 ml/2 cups hot water. Add salt to taste.

Bring to the boil, then add the tofu and 'scallop balls' (if using). If you want to make the soup a little spicy, add the chillies/chiles. The broth evaporates easily and you want plenty to cover the noodles and vegetables, so add more water if needed. Bring to the boil, then set aside. Remove the lemongrass.

Put a large handful of noodles in each serving bowl, then ladle over the soup, ensuring there is a mixture of vegetables and tofu in each bowl, and the liquid covers almost all the noodles. Sprinkle over the beansprouts, coriander/cilantro and sliced chillies/chiles, then add a squeeze of lime juice.

ROYAL LAOS TOM YUM WITH FIVE-SPICE TOFU & STICKY RICE BALLS

I developed this recipe while reading books about food in Laos, where a handful of rice is added to the Royal Laos version of this soup. We often enjoyed some of the best sticky rice in Laos and Eastern Thailand, where you can dip the lovely sticky ball into a fragrant yellow curry or broth. These sticky balls are the perfect accompaniment to any dish with a good broth, so I think they work well here. Laotians and Thais make their sticky rice by steaming in bamboo baskets or tubes. You can buy these easily at an Asian supermarket, and they do add something to the flavour of the rice. But I also use the stove-top method (page 13) when I'm cooking for larger numbers, and it produces a good consistency in the stickiness of the rice. Just be accurate with your measurements.

6 lemongrass stalks, finely sliced

5-cm/2-in. piece of galangal or root ginger, peeled and finely chopped

6 kaffir lime leaves

250 g/9 oz. firm tofu, rinsed, drained, excess water squeezed out and cut into 2-cm/¾-in. cubes

½ teaspoon Chinese five-spice powder

a bunch of fresh coriander/cilantro stems, finely chopped

100 ml/scant ½ cup tamarind pulp or paste, or 1 teaspoon tamarind concentrate

2–4 fresh bird's eye chillies/chiles, to taste, or 2 large red chillies/chiles, thinly sliced

2 tablespoons vegan fish sauce (page 13), or 1 tablespoon light soy sauce and a pinch of seaweed flakes

80 g/heaped ⅓ cup soft brown sugar

2 tablespoons soy sauce

16 cherry tomatoes, halved

8 vegan 'prawns/shrimp' or 'scallop balls' (optional)

freshly squeezed juice of 2 limes

a handful of fresh coriander/cilantro leaves

a handful of fresh holy basil, leaves

lime wedges, to serve

salt, to taste

STICKY RICE

400 g/scant 2 cups glutinous rice, soaked in water for 2 hours or overnight

1 teaspoon salt

baking sheet, greased

SERVES 4

Cook the sticky rice according to the packet instructions or the advice on page 13.

Preheat the oven to 180°C (350°F) Gas 4.

Pound the lemongrass, galangal and lime leaves in a mortar using a pestle to make a rough pulp. Set aside.

Lay the tofu cubes on the prepared baking sheet and dust all over with the five-spice powder. Season with salt and bake in the oven for 15–20 minutes until golden and crispy. Set aside.

Put 1 litre/4⅓ cups water in a large pan over high heat and bring to the boil. Add the lemongrass mixture, the coriander/cilantro stems, tamarind and chillies/chiles. Bring to the boil and simmer for 5–6 minutes.

Add the vegan fish sauce, followed by the sugar and soy sauce, then add the tomatoes, 'prawns/shrimp' (if using), baked tofu and the lime juice. Bring back to the boil and then remove from the heat.

Roll the sticky rice into balls, and put onto side plates. Pour the soup into bowls and top with a few coriander/cilantro and basil leaves. Serve with the sticky rice balls and lime wedges.

BANH MI BUDDHA

VIETNAMESE STUFFED BAGUETTE WITH GOCHUJANG TOFU, ROASTED MUSHROOM PÂTÉ AND PICKLED VEG

We never got to sample a true banh mi when we were travelling, because the only version we ever saw was stuffed with pork. I desperately wanted to try a veggie version, so I created this one especially for my own street food menu. We served this on the MasterChef street food bus during the summer in 2014, and the feedback was incredible from meat-eaters, veggies and vegans. This may only be a sandwich at heart, but it's one mighty snack of a sandwich. The pâté will keep for a week in the fridge, the chilli sambal will keep for a month, and the vegetable pickles will keep for up to a year in a sterilized jar. The chilli/chile sambal doesn't blend well in a food processor if you try to make it in small quantities, so it's better to make larger amounts and keep it in the fridge for using another time, or make a smaller amount than given here and use a pestle and mortar.

1 French-style thick
   baguette or 4 mini
   baguettes
mixed lettuce leaves,
   fresh coriander/cilantro
   leaves, Thai basil oil
   (optional), to serve

PICKLES
250–300g/1¼–1½ cups
   caster/superfine sugar
1 litre/4⅓ cups rice
   vinegar
½ teaspoon black
   peppercorns
½ teaspoon Szechuan
   peppercorns
1 cucumber, halved
   lengthways
1 daikon/mooli, peeled
2 carrots

MUSHROOM PÂTÉ
80 g/heaped ½ cup
   walnuts, lightly toasted
10 field mushrooms
2 tablespoons coconut oil
a handful of fresh flat-leaf
   parsley leaves
salt and ground white
   pepper, to taste

MAPLE CHILLI SAMBAL
500 g/1lb. 2oz. large red
   chillies/chiles, trimmed
1 garlic bulb, broken into
   cloves, unpeeled
60 ml/¼ cup pomace oil,
   or vegetable oil
2 tablespoons soft dark
   brown sugar, or to taste
2 tablespoons light soy
   sauce, or tamari
1 tablespoon Sherry or
   Shaoxing (optional)
2 tablespoons maple
   syrup
1 teaspoon salt,
   or to taste

TOFU
1 heaped tablespoon
   Korean red pepper/
   bell pepper paste
   (gochujang)
2 teaspoons toasted
   sesame oil
2 tablespoons light soy
   sauce
400 g/14 oz. firm tofu,
   rinsed, drained and
   cut into 4-cm/1½-in.
   flat squares

3 baking sheets, greased

SERVES 4

Preheat the oven to 180°C (350°F) Gas 4.

To make the pickles, put 240 ml/1 cup water in a pan over medium heat and add 250 g/1¼ cups of the sugar, the vinegar and both types of peppercorns. Stir and bring to the boil. Taste the liquid and add more sugar, if needed, to achieve a well-balanced sweet-and-sour tang.

Meanwhile, using a teaspoon, scrape out the watery seeds from the centre of the cucumber. Using a vegetable peeler, slice the cucumber, daikon/mooli and carrots to make thin ribbons. Put the vegetable ribbons in the pan of hot liquid and then remove it from the heat. Stir well and leave to cool. Store immediately in a sterilized glass jar for up to 1 year.

To make the pâté, place the walnuts on a baking sheet and bake in the preheated oven for about 10–12 minutes, until lightly toasted. Remove from the oven and set aside. Reduce the oven to 120°C (250°F) Gas ½.

Put the mushrooms in a roasting pan and cook in the oven for 30–40 minutes, until the mushrooms are well roasted and fairly dry in appearance, occasionally draining away the liquid from the pan. Put the mushrooms into a food processor or blender and add the walnuts and all the remaining ingredients, then blend until smooth. Season with salt and pepper to taste. Increase the oven temperature to 220°C (425°F) Gas 7.

To make the sambal, put the chillies/chiles on one prepared baking sheet and the garlic cloves on another. Bake the chillies/chiles for 10–15 minutes until they are well roasted and starting to blacken at the edges; bake the garlic for 8–10 minutes until golden brown and sticky. Reduce the oven temperature to 180°C (350°F) Gas 4.

Peel the garlic cloves and put them in a food processor or blender with the chillies/chiles and all the remaining ingredients, then blend until smooth. Adjust the sugar and salt to taste – this is a very spicy sauce but it should have a sweet edge.

To make the tofu, put all the ingredients, except the tofu, in a shallow bowl and mix to make a marinade. Add the tofu and coat in the marinade. Put the tofu on a prepared baking sheet and bake in the oven for 30 minutes or until starting to crisp around edges. Keep warm.

Cut the baguette into quarters, then slice in half horizontally, leaving a hinge at the side. Using your fingers, scoop out some of the crumb from the centre. Spread the maple chilli/chile sambal thinly on one side of the bread. Spread the mushroom pâté thickly on the other side. Half-fill the bread with mixed leaves, if using, then lay 3 or 4 pieces of warm tofu overlapping down the centre.

Take a forkful of pickles and layer it across the top, using the fork to push the fillings into the bread so that it's well stuffed. Finish with a few more pickles, some fresh coriander/cilantro and a drizzle of basil oil, if using, on top. Serve immediately.

LOTUS SALAD

The stem or root of the aquatic lotus plant is very popular in salads in Vietnam. It's also delicious used in Indian koftas or grated into Thai style patties, as it has tremendous bite even after cooking. It is worth hunting out some Vietnamese mint (rau ram) for this dish. They often use blanched young cabbage or lettuce leaves to make wraps out of this salad in Vietnam (and Laos), as well as turning it into summer rolls using rice paper. However, I think this salad is delicious served on its own.

200 g/7 oz. fresh lotus stem or bulb, thinly sliced
vegetable oil, for shallow-frying
1 banana shallot, thinly sliced
freshly squeezed juice of 2 limes
1 tablespoon kecap manis (Indonesian sweet soy sauce)
½ teaspoon caster/superfine sugar, or to taste
1 tablespoon rice vinegar
½ teaspoon sesame oil
¼ teaspoon salt, or to taste
a large handful of fresh holy basil or a mixture of mint and European basil leaves, chopped
1 carrot, cut into thin sticks
½ daikon/mooli, peeled and cut into thin sticks
2–3 tofu puffs, sliced into thin sticks
2 spring onions/scallions, thinly sliced at an angle
1 large red chilli/chile, thinly sliced at an angle
1 tablespoon roasted peanuts, chopped (optional)
Vietnamese mint leaves or fresh coriander/cilantro, to garnish

SERVES 2–3

Bring a large saucepan of water to the boil and add the lotus stem. Blanch for 3–4 minutes, or until tender then drain in a colander and refresh under cold water. Drain again and set aside.

Heat the oil in a pan over medium heat and cook the shallot for 10 minutes until deep brown and crispy. Drain on paper towels and set aside.

Put the lime juice in a large bowl with the kecap manis, sugar, rice vinegar, sesame oil and salt and stir until all the sugar has dissolved. Taste to check the balance of seasoning, and add more salt or sugar if needed.

Add the blanched lotus root, basil, carrot, daikon/mooli, tofu sticks, spring onions/scallions and chilli/chile. Mix gently with your hands until all the salad is well coated in dressing.

Divide the salad between serving plates and scatter the top with the chopped roasted peanuts, if using, and crispy shallots. Finish with some fresh Vietnamese mint leaves or coriander/cilantro leaves before serving.

STUFFED BETEL LEAVES WITH RICE PAPER FRITTERS & GINGER-LIME DIP

Young betel leaves are delicious with a variety of fillings. You will find them in the fridge in a good Chinese or a South-east Asian supermarket. I've enjoyed them like little Thai tacos filled with a spicy pomelo salad, and in Vietnam they are often stuffed and griddled (with beef). This recipe uses meaty mushrooms, with savoury and zesty dips to crank up the flavour. Rice paper fritters puff up best if you can leave them overnight to dry.

3 lemongrass stalks, white part only, finely chopped

1 small red onion or shallot, peeled and quartered

2 garlic cloves, peeled

2 tablespoons vegetable oil 250 g/9 oz. oyster mushrooms, roughly chopped, or substitute Portobello or field mushrooms

3 tablespoons vegan fish sauce (page 13)

1 teaspoon caster/superfine sugar

1 tablespoon garam masala

½ teaspoon ground black pepper

¼ teaspoon salt

16 betel leaves, or substitute fresh beetroot/beet leaves

a handful of fresh mint, basil and coriander/cilantro leaves, to serve

2 Thai red chillies/chiles, deep-fried, to serve (optional)

a handful of toasted and chopped peanuts, (optional)

RICE PAPER FRITTERS
18 rice papers

400 ml/1¾ cups vegetable oil, for deep-frying

GINGER-LIME DIP
1 Thai chilli/chile, finely chopped

2 tablespoons soft brown sugar

1 garlic clove, crushed and finely chopped

3 tablespoons vegan fish sauce (page 13)

freshly squeezed juice of 3 limes

2 kaffir lime leaves, finely sliced (optional)

8-cm/3-¼in. piece of root ginger, finely chopped

SPRING ONION/SCALLION DIPPING OIL
2 spring onions/scallions, thinly sliced and lightly toasted in a dry frying pan/skillet for 10–15 seconds

240 ml/1 cup pomace oil, or vegetable oil

4 bamboo skewers

SERVES 2–4

Soak the rice papers (one at a time) in hand-hot water until softened. Lay six sheets on top of each other, gently pressing down to flatten. Repeat, using all the rice papers. Using a sharp knife, cut into 4-cm/1½-in. squares and then press down hard on the edges of the squares. Set aside to dry out for 3–4 hours, or overnight.

Pound the lemongrass, onion and garlic in a mortar using a pestle to make a rough pulp.

Heat the 2 tablespoons of oil in a pan and fry the lemongrass mixture for 5–6 minutes until translucent. Add the mushrooms, vegan fish sauce, sugar, garam masala, pepper and salt, and fry gently for 3–4 minutes. Set aside to cool.

Combine all the ingredients for the ginger-lime dip and set aside for 40 minutes. Combine all the spring onion/scallion dipping oil ingredients and set aside.

In a large pan, heat the vegetable oil for deep-frying the rice paper fritters to medium-hot, about 190°C (375°F). Fry the squares until they puff up and become crisp, then set aside on paper towels to dry.

Lay the betel leaves vein-side up, and add a tablespoon of the stuffing mixture into the centre of each leaf. Fold in the sides and roll up like a spring roll. Thread onto a bamboo skewer. Repeat, placing 4–5 stuffed leaves onto each skewer. These rolls can be served with the filling still warm and also can be briefly griddled, to wilt the leaves, as preferred.

Serve immediately with the dipping sauce and dipping oil, crispy rice paper fritters, fresh herbs, fried chillies/chiles and toasted peanuts (if using).

NAM ROM KHO TO
MUSHROOM CLAYPOT

The claypot is mostly known as a dish of Chinese origin; however, this dish is based on the Vietnamese dish, straw mushroom claypot. It's impossible to source fresh straw mushrooms in the UK, so I use oyster and chestnut mushrooms instead. I do like the unusual taste and texture of straw mushrooms, so I add canned ones to the mix. For such a simple dish, this certainly packs plenty of savoury flavour too. Less than 15 minutes to prepare, this is a popular midweek family favourite in our house.

½ tablespoon vegetable oil

2 garlic cloves, crushed and finely chopped

120 g/4 oz. whole straw mushrooms, drained and rinsed if canned

120 g/4 oz. chestnut mushrooms, quartered

120 g/4 oz. oyster mushrooms, roughly torn

4 tablespoons soy sauce or tamari

2 tablespoons soft brown sugar, or agave syrup

½ teaspoon salt, or to taste

1 teaspoon freshly ground black pepper, or to taste

steamed rice, to serve

sliced radish and spring onions/scallions, to serve

SERVES 2–3

Put a heat-proof claypot or large pan over medium heat and add the oil. Cook the garlic for 3 minutes or until it starts to soften. Add all the mushrooms and cook for a further 1 minute, stirring.

Add all the remaining ingredients to the pan with 2–3 tablespoons water, then cover and simmer over low heat for 10 minutes. Remove the lid and check the seasoning.

Serve with steamed rice and a simple crunchy salad of sliced radishes and spring onions/scallions.

GINGER & LEMONGRASS ICED TEA

This refreshing drink reminds me of sitting on the banks of the Mekong watching the children swim in the river. Marika's father, an ex-US serviceman, used to make these for us when it was too hot to do anything other than perfect the art of doing nothing.

2–4 teaspoons sugar, to taste, or agave syrup

1 lemongrass stalk, crushed

5-cm/2-in. piece of fresh ginger, peeled and thinly sliced

3–4 teaspoons green tea leaves or 5 tea bags

ice cubes, to serve

lime wedges, to serve

SERVES 4–6

Half-fill a medium pan with boiling water and add 2 teaspoons of the sugar, the lemongrass and ginger. Simmer for 10 minutes. Check the level of sweetness and adjust to taste.

Add the tea and remove from the heat. Allow to infuse/steep for 4–5 minutes until it is brewed to your taste. Using a very fine strainer, strain the liquid into a jug/pitcher and leave to cool, then put it in the fridge for 2–3 hours to chill. Serve in tall glasses with plenty of ice, lime wedges and drinking straws.

MALAYSIA & INDONESIA

Malaysia

GEORGETOWN, PENANG Malaysian food, like the country itself, is a melting pot of Chinese, Indian and Thai food, as well as their own unique dishes. It is also home to some of the greatest street food in the world. The island of Penang, and its colonial capital Georgetown, has the most amazing street food markets and cafés, and we never failed to find something delicious to eat there. If there were seven wonders of the street food world, I think Georgetown in Penang would definitely be one of them.

The island sits off the north-west corner of peninsula Malaysia, where the Andaman sea becomes the Straits of Malacca. Georgetown reflects Penang's history of trading routes, immigration and colonialism with magnificent architecture and numerous multi-cultural quarters to explore. Lee and I first visited the island in 1994 on an overland trip to Sumatra and we loved it immediately. We stayed in a simple hostel and over two days we ate food from all corners of Asia. Steamed dumplings, banana leaf thali, crispy dosas, spicy fritters and skewers, noodle soups and lassi like nectar. It's not difficult to find vegetarian cafés and street food vendors, especially in Georgetown.

We spent a month driving around the peninsular, where we discovered that fish heads were very common, and vegetarianism less so (especially on the east coast). We had some great eating experiences in cities like Ipoh, Melaka and Kuala Lumpur, or tourist areas like the Cameron Highlands. Fortunately the country was so beautiful, it distracted us from our sometimes mainland diet of roti canai for every meal. The east coast islands give Thailand's a run for their money with crystal blue water and fascinating sea life, but we were forced to eat far too many eggs and a lot of peanut butter crackers. While many Malay dishes were far from vegan or vegetarian, I found myself hankering for the aromatic spices I could smell. On returning home, I started to study Malaysian dishes and how they could be adjusted to create something we could all eat.

From left to right: Street food market, Penang; Cycle rickshaw Kuan Yin Teng temple, Georgetown; Giant incense sticks, Goddess of Mercy Temple; Chinese lanterns, Penang; Site of the Georgetown World Heritage Building, Penang; Coral beach sunset, Perhentian Kecil; Steam boat dinner, Tanah Rata, Cameron Highlands.

ROTI CANAI
VEGETABLE DAL WITH FLAKY FLATBREAD

This is the vegan dish you will find on most Malaysian street corners, eaten for breakfast or as a snack. The dal varies depending on where you are. It is sometimes substantial and rich, with yellow split channa and plenty of seasonal vegetables, flavoured with coconut and tamarind (such as the one detailed here) or a thinner Tamil-style toor dal called Sambar Dal (page 63). But it's the roti bread (the same flaky bread known as parotta in southern India and Sri Lanka, or flaky paratha in UK) with its all-at-the-same-time flaky crispy softness that had us coming back time and again. It is possible to buy a decent frozen version in Asian supermarkets, but it's always fun to have a go at something. To be fair, the roti makers have grown up doing this and honed this skill to an art form. I'm not ashamed to admit I have made some terrible versions. The simple Sri Lankan parotta recipe (p82) is used here, and if all else fails, check out the freezer section in your local Asian grocers. The dal recipe is based on ones we enjoyed during our tour of the Malay peninsular. As we drove up the East coast, our stop offs for food were awash with fish head curry so we relied on this substantial vegetable dal to keep us going. One of my favourites was served in a café attached to a laundrette in Kuala Terangganu. Served with a perfectly flaki roti of course.

200 g/1 cup yellow split peas (split channa)
1 teaspoon ground turmeric
1 aubergine/eggplant, cut into bite-sized pieces
1 large onion, chopped
4 tomatoes, diced
1 carrot, diced
1 large waxy/red potato, cubed
1 small green chilli/chile, finely chopped
200 ml/scant 1 cup coconut milk
½ teaspoon tamarind concentrate, or 1 tablespoon tamarind pulp or paste
salt and freshly ground black pepper
Parotta (Flaky Roti Bread), to serve (page 82)

TEMPERING
2 tablespoons vegetable oil
1 small red onion, finely chopped
4 garlic cloves, thinly sliced
1 teaspoon mustard seeds
1 teaspoon cumin seeds
1 small green chilli/chile, finely chopped
a handful of fresh or dried curry leaves

SERVES 4–6

Put the yellow split peas in a large, heavy pan and cover generously with water. Bring to the boil over high heat, then add the turmeric and boil for 10 minutes. Using a slotted spoon, remove the frothy scum. Add the aubergine/eggplant to the pan followed by the other vegetables and the chopped chilli/chile, then add 570ml/2½ cups boiling water. Bring back to the boil and simmer for 15–20 minutes or until the vegetables are soft and it is the consistency of porridge (add more hot water if needed). Stir in the coconut milk and tamarind, and add salt to taste.

For the tempering, put the oil in a small frying pan/skillet and fry the red onion and garlic for 6–8 minutes, until golden. Add the mustard and cumin seeds and the remaining tempering ingredients. Fry for a further 2–3 minutes. Pour the tempering over the dal and stir. Taste and add more salt if needed. Serve the dal with the flaky roti bread/parotta.

ASSAM LAKSA
PENANG HOT-AND-SOUR NOODLE SOUP

There are lots of great vegetarian cafés in Penang, and many offer their own version of a vegetarian Assam/Penang laksa – a much-famed dish on the island. My recipe relies on a home-made vegan fish sauce or a pinch of seaweed flakes to add flavour to this popular hot-and-sour noodle broth, usually made with Indian mackerel. I use paprika and roast large fresh chillies/chiles to bring colour and depth of flavour. I also use the much underrated lotus root, with its unique, crunchy texture. Buy fresh ones from a Chinese grocer, or substitute sliced water chestnuts.

6 red chillies/chiles, stems removed
2 small red onions, unpeeled and halved
2 lemongrass stalks
1 tablespoon paprika
vegetable oil, if needed
1 litre/quart vegetable stock
3 tablespoons vegan fish sauce (page 13), or light soy sauce with a pinch of seaweed flakes
2 tablespoons tamarind pulp, or 2 teaspoons tamarind concentrate/ paste
1–2 teaspoons salt, to taste
1–2 tablespoons soft brown sugar, or rice syrup, to taste

375 g/13 oz. thick round rice noodles or egg- free yellow noodles

FRESH TOPPINGS
½ cucumber, halved lengthways
1 fresh lotus root, peeled
½ pineapple
a handful of Vietnamese mint leaves, or a mixture of mint and European basil leaves
a handful of laksa leaves
1 small red onion, thinly sliced
1 bird's eye chilli/chile, finely chopped

SERVES 4–6

Preheat the oven to 210°C (410°F) Gas 6.

Put the chillies/chiles and onions on a baking sheet and roast for 10–15 minutes until starting to blacken at the edges. Let cool, then peel the onions.

Put the lemongrass in a food processor and add the paprika, roasted chillies and onions, then blend to a paste, adding a little oil if needed to thin the mixture. Put the spice paste in a wok or large pan over high heat and cook for 2 minutes.

Add the stock, 1 litre/quart water, the vegan fish sauce and tamarind to the pan. Bring to the boil over high heat and simmer briskly for 8–10 minutes. Add salt and sugar to taste.

Meanwhile, soak the noodles in hot water for 10 minutes, then drain in a colander.

To prepare the fresh toppings, using a teaspoon, scrape out the watery seeds from the centre of the cucumber. Thinly slice the cucumber and lotus root. Blanch the sliced lotus root in boiling water for 1 minute, then set aside. Using a sharp knife, cut the top and bottom off the pineapple, then stand it on one end and cut off the peel and the 'eyes'. Cut the pineapple in half lengthways and cut out the core. Chop the flesh.

Divide the noodles among serving bowls, then add a selection of the fresh toppings. Ladle over the broth to ensure the noodles are well covered. Serve.

BUDDHA'S TAPAS

HOISIN MOCK DUCK AND CHILLI/CHILE-BEAN TOFU LETTUCE CUPS WITH STEAMED FLOWER BUNS

This dish was inspired by Fat Yan's, our all-time favourite vegetarian restaurant in Kuala Lumpur, run by a Buddhist Chinese family. Unfortunately, a standard Chinese restaurant has now replaced the old restaurant, but at least we were lucky enough to visit the old place numerous times when passing through KL (which we often used as a hub to reach the more far-flung corners of Malaysia and Indonesia). Our favourite dishes included the sticky 'mock' spare ribs, stuffed steamed buns and lettuce wraps, although I'm pretty sure we ate the entire menu and were never once disappointed.

I created this dish especially for my menu at the Manchester International Festival in 2013, using Fuchsia Dunlop's recipe for steamed flower rolls. I had some black sea salt I wanted to try in a dish that it wouldn't get lost in, and this seemed the perfect opportunity to pair the salt with Sichuan peppercorns. It all turned out to be a bit too complicated to serve for the high numbers of a festival in the end (so I rarely serve this from my street food menu these days). But the diners loved it, and I still think it's a fabulous dish that makes a stunning dining plate. It's worth the effort for a special occasion and you can add the Baked Spring Rolls (page 177) and Slow-baked Crispy Kale (page 200) to the selection platter too. The tangy hoi sin and chilli bean heat are complemented by lots of texture from the tofu, seitan and crunchy lettuce. If you can't get pickled mustard greens, you can make your own vegetable pickles (page 143) that will also balance the flavours well.

2 Little Gem/Bibb or mini Romaine lettuces
100-g/3½-oz. packet of preserved mustard greens (optional), to serve

SALT AND PEPPER STEAMED BUNS
½ teaspoon sugar
½ tablespoon active dried yeast
250 g/2 cups plain/all-purpose flour, plus extra to dust
a splash of groundnut/peanut oil, plus extra to grease
1 tablespoon sea salt flakes (use black or coloured if you can find them)
1 tablespoon Sichuan peppercorns

CHILLI/CHILE-BEAN FILLING
2 tablespoons groundnut/peanut or vegetable oil
2 slices mock bacon (optional), chopped into small pieces, or soy-marinated tempeh
400 g/14 oz. firm tofu, rinsed, drained and chopped into 2-cm/¾-in. pieces

1 tablespoon chilli/chile bean paste
1 teaspoon Sichuan sweet bean paste
2 teaspoon fermented black beans
1 teaspoon dark soy sauce
1 teaspoon caster/superfine sugar
6 baby leeks, thinly sliced at an angle
sea salt (optional)

HOISIN SEITAN FILLING
280-g/10-oz. can seitan (mock duck or chicken made from gluten), washed and shredded
4 tablespoons hoisin sauce
½ cucumber
6 spring onions/scallions, cut in half, then thinly sliced lengthways

baking sheet, lightly greased

SERVES 4–6

To make the buns, put the sugar and yeast in a bowl and add 125ml/½ cup lukewarm water, then leave in a warm place for 15 minutes until frothy.

Put the flour in a large bowl and make a well in the centre. Pour in the yeast mixture, with 2 tablespoons warm water. Mix well to form a soft dough, then knead the dough vigorously on a floured work surface for 10 minutes. Put in a well-oiled bowl, cover with a damp dish towel and leave in a warm place for 2 hours or until the dough has doubled in size. Lightly knead again to knock out the air. Leave for another 30 minutes.

Put the dough on a floured surface and knead again for a few minutes. Then roll the dough into a long, wide sausage shape about 20 cm/8 in. wide. Brush the surface with a small amount of oil, then sprinkle lightly with about 1 teaspoon each of sea salt flakes and Sichuan peppercorns – just enough of a scatter for a pop of flavour here and there.

Roll out the dough to make a long, thin Swiss roll/jelly roll shape and pinch each end to seal. Using a sharp knife, cut into 2-cm/¾-in. slices. Lay the slices on the work surface and, using a pair of chopsticks, squeeze the opposite sides of each roll together slightly, to make a loose figure-of-eight. Sprinkle 2 peppercorns and salt flakes onto each.

Put in a lightly oiled steamer and then steam for 10 minutes until fully risen and cooked. Preheat the oven to 200°C (400°F) Gas 6.

For the lettuce cups, trim the ends of the lettuces and gently remove the whole outer leaves, then set aside for later.

To make the chilli-bean filling, heat 1 tablespoon of the oil in a small frying pan/skillet and cook the mock bacon, if using, until golden brown. Set aside

on paper towels. Add another ½ tablespoon of the oil and fry the tofu in batches until crispy and brown on the outside. Set aside on paper towels.

To make the hoisin seitan filling, put the seitan in a small bowl and add 2 tablespoons of the hoisin sauce. Leave to marinate for 20 minutes. Lay the mock duck on the prepared baking sheet in one layer, then bake for 10–15 minutes until the seitan is starting to crisp and tastes chewy.

Using a teaspoon, scrape out the watery seeds from the centre of the cucumber. Cut the flesh into fine matchsticks and set aside.

Heat a wok over medium heat, add the remaining ½ tablespoon oil for the chilli-bean cups, then add the chilli/chile bean paste, the sweet bean paste and fermented black beans. Stir-fry for a few minutes, and then add the soy sauce and sugar. Check the seasoning and add salt if necessary, but it shouldn't need it as the black beans are salty.

Add the fried tofu and mock bacon, if using, and cook for 1 minute, then add the baby leeks and cook until the leeks are just softening. Set aside until ready to serve.

To serve, lay 4 lettuce cups onto each plate, and half-fill 2 lettuce cups with hoisin seitan filling and two with the chilli-bean filling. Top each of the hoisin seitan lettuce cups with a pinch of sliced spring onions/scallions and cucumber slivers, then drizzle with a little of the remaining hoisin sauce. Add a steamed bun to each serving and serve each with a teaspoon of preserved mustard greens, if you like.

NONYA DUMPLINGS

BAMBOO-WRAPPED RICE DUMPLINGS WITH SAVOURY TEMPEH STUFFING

These bamboo-leaf-wrapped sticky rice dumplings are a common street food in Malaysia, Singapore and Indonesia. They're an example of Nonya or Peranakan cooking, a Chinese and Malaysian-influenced style, so they tend to be called Nonya dumplings (and are sometimes coloured blue using pea flowers!). The problem for a non-meat eater is that you never know what might be inside them, unless you happen to be where the vendor understands some English or you speak enough Bahasa to have a vague chance of being understood (which we discovered was not at a street stall at a remote bus stop in Borneo!). We ended up trying them in Penang, where they had a sweet, red bean filling, and then a number of port towns in Indonesia, where they were often stuffed with tempeh. They were the perfectly packaged portable snack for taking on the boat.

350 g/1¾ cups glutinous rice
50 g/3½ tablespoons coconut oil, or vegetable oil
4 star anise
7.5-cm/3-in. piece of cassia bark
2 teaspoons salt
1 teaspoon ground white pepper
16 whole bamboo leaves (dried, fresh or frozen)
5 pandan leaves, rinsed and cut into 4–5-cm/1½–2-in. strips
Simple Sambal (page 33) or Pickled Cucumber Salad (page 167), to serve

FILLING
6 dried Chinese mushrooms
1 tablespoon vegetable oil
1 small red onion or shallot, finely chopped
4 garlic cloves, crushed
180 g/6½ oz. tempeh, roughly chopped
1½ tablespoons ground coriander
1½ tablespoons sweet dark soy sauce
1½ tablespoons light soy sauce
1–2 teaspoons soft brown sugar, to taste
½ teaspoon salt, or to taste

½ teaspoon freshly ground black pepper
a pinch of star anise powder (optional)
1 tablespoon dried blue pea flowers (optional)

twine or grass strands, to tie the dumplings

MAKES 18–20 DUMPLINGS

Wash the glutinous rice several times until the water runs clear, then soak it in cold water overnight. Rinse again and leave to drain in a sieve/strainer. Soak the mushrooms for the filling in hot water for 20 minutes, then drain and finely chop them. Set aside.

Put the coconut oil in a heavy-based pan over medium heat and add the star anise, cassia bark, salt and white pepper. Fry gently for 2–3 minutes, but do not cook. Stir well and remove from the heat. Remove the star anise and cassia bark.

To make the filling, heat the oil in a frying pan/skillet and cook the onion for 5 minutes or until softened and translucent. Add the garlic and mushrooms, then cook for 3–4 minutes. Add the remaining ingredients, except the blue pea flowers, and 2 tablespoons water, and simmer gently for 5–10 minutes, until there is still a little liquid in the mixture, but not too much. Check the flavour balance of salty and sweetness, and adjust as necessary. Remove from the heat and let cool.

Prepare the bamboo leaves and grass strands (if using dried), by boiling them for 20–30 minutes, then drain and let cool. Wipe each leaf gently, whether using dried, fresh or frozen, and set aside.

Fold each bamboo leaf at the centre fold to form a cone, then partly fill with some of the rice (and a dried blue pea flower, if using), making a small well with rice around the bottom and sides. Spoon a tablespoonful of the filling into the centre of each, then top with some more rice to cover the filling. Remember that the rice will increase in volume during cooking, so don't put too much in.

Put a pandan strip over the top of the rice, then tightly wrap the bamboo leaf around the cone, to form a triangular pouch, 5–6 cm/2–2½ in. long. Secure with twine or grass strands. Leave a loop on each to make them easier to drain after cooking. Drop the pouches into boiling water, and simmer for 2 hours. Remove and hang to dry for another hour or so. Serve with sambal or pickled cucumber salad.

VEGETARIAN MEE REBUS
SWEET POTATO AND SOYA/SOY BEAN NOODLE CURRY

Mee rebus is a popular noodle dish across Malaysia, Indonesia and Singapore and is another example of Peranakan or Nonya cooking. It is slightly sweet and deeply savoury with a silky curry-like sauce containing sweet potato, tomato and soya/soy bean paste. Commonly served with boiled eggs, this dish works well as a vegan dish too. Although normally served with 'hokkien' yellow noodles, which contain egg, it is possible to find yellow egg-free noodles at Chinese supermarkets or use fermented kanom jeen rice noodles. Crispy shallots bring a key sweet, crisp note. I make a large batch and store in an airtight container.

6 large dried red chillies/
  chiles, soaked in hot
  water for 20 minutes
  and drained
5-cm/2-in. piece of
  galangal, peeled
  and chopped, or
  1 tablespoon ground
  galangal
2 small fresh turmeric
  roots, peeled, or
  1 teaspoon ground
  turmeric
4 garlic cloves, chopped
120 ml/½ cup, plus
  1–2 tablespoons
  vegetable oil
2 tablespoons brown
  soya/soy bean paste
1 red onion, diced
2 all-purpose potatoes,
  such as Maris Piper/
  Yukon gold, chopped
2 sweet potatoes,
  chopped
1.2 litres/5 cups
  vegetable stock
3 ripe tomatoes, cored
  and chopped
1–2 teaspoons salt,
  to taste

½–1 tablespoon soft
  brown sugar, to taste
8 tofu puffs, quartered
8 cherry tomatoes, halved
375-g/13-oz. packet of
  egg-free yellow
  noodles, kanom jeen
  noodles or thick round
  rice noodles
1 small bunch of Chinese
  celery leaves, chopped,
  or 1 bunch of spring
  onions/scallions
2 large green chillies/
  chiles, thinly sliced
1 lime, cut into wedges

**CRISPY SHALLOTS
AND CHILLIES**
500 ml/2 cups vegetable
  oil, for frying
2 banana shallots, thinly
  sliced
2 large red chillies/chiles,
  thinly sliced

SERVES 2–3

Put the chillies/chiles in a food processor or blender and add the galangal, turmeric, garlic, onion, soya/soy bean paste and the 120 ml/½ cup oil. Blend to make a smooth paste. (Alternatively, use a pestle and mortar or finely chop, as it will be blended again later.)

Boil the white potatoes in water to cover for 10 minutes or until tender, then drain. Heat the 1–2 tablespoons oil in a large wok or pan and add the spice paste. Cook for 3 minutes, stirring. Add the sweet potatoes, stock and chopped tomatoes. Bring to the boil, then simmer for 10–15 minutes or until the sweet potatoes are soft, then add the cooked white potatoes. Bring back to the boil, then remove from the heat.

Using a food processor or blender, process the mixture until silky smooth. Add the salt and sugar to taste. Add the tofu puffs and cherry tomatoes. Bring back to the boil, then remove from the heat.

For the crispy shallots and chillies, heat the oil in a pan over high heat. Test the temperature by dropping in a shallot – if it sizzles, it's ready. Add the shallots and chillies/chiles and fry until the sizzling diminishes and they are golden brown. Remove from the pan, drain on paper towels and set aside.

Cook the noodles according to the packet instructions, then drain and divide between serving bowls. Ladle the sauce over and top with Chinese celery, green chillies/chiles, crispy shallots and chillies/chiles, and wedges of lime.

SWEET PEANUT SOUP

LOTUS ROOT AND PEANUT BROTH WITH SAVOURY STUFFED MOCHI DUMPLING

Peanut soups are common in Malaysian food, some are savoury-based with pork ribs and lotus root, and others are sweet versions with steamed yam and sweet potato, which weren't really my cup of tea. Peanut and lotus root soup is traditionally eaten for Chinese New Year, and it's these ingredients that represent its lucky charms for wealth (peanuts) and abundance (lotus root). This vegan version is my fusion recipe, using Japanese-style rice dumplings called mochi.

2 dried shiitake
   mushrooms
4 large dates,
   stoned/pitted
100 g/¾ cup peanuts
1 fresh lotus root, peeled
   and thickly sliced
1 tablespoon vegan fish
   sauce, or light soy
   sauce and a pinch
   of seaweed flakes
Vietnamese lemon mint
   leaves, to garnish
   (optional)

DUMPLINGS
2 dried Chinese
   mushrooms
200 g/1½ cups glutinous
   rice flour, plus extra if
   needed and to dust
25 g/2 tablespoons mung
   beans, soaked
   overnight and drained
¼ teaspoon Chinese
   five-spice powder
a pinch of salt

SERVES 2–3

Put the shiitake mushrooms and the Chinese mushrooms for the dumplings in separate bowls and cover with hot water. Leave for 20 minutes, then drain both and slice the shiitake mushrooms thinly, and chop the Chinese mushrooms finely. Set the Chinese mushrooms aside. Put 1 litre/quart water in a large pan over high heat and add the shiitake mushrooms, dates, peanuts, lotus root and vegan fish sauce, then bring to the boil, reduce the heat and simmer for 40–50 minutes.

Meanwhile, to make the dumplings, put the rice flour in a bowl and add 6 tablespoons hot water, then stir to combine. Add a tiny amount of flour if the dough is too sticky to handle, then knead it gently so that it comes together to make a soft, pliable dough. Divide and roll the dough on a floured work surface into grape-sized balls.

Put the mung beans in a pan and cover generously with water, then bring to the boil and simmer for 30–40 minutes or until soft. Drain in a colander and return the beans to the pan, then mash them to a fine paste. Add the Chinese mushrooms to the mung bean paste with the five-spice powder and salt. Mix together well.

Take a dumpling ball and, using a fingertip, poke an indentation into it. Fill with a little of the mushroom paste, then re-roll the dumpling ball to seal it. Repeat with the remaining dumpling balls and mushroom paste. Put the dumplings into the simmering peanut broth, and boil until they rise to the surface (about 4 minutes). Serve immediately, garnished with Vietnamese mint leaves, if you like.

The murtabak stall is nearly always found alongside the roti canai stall (I think they share the dough). Here they prepared the delicious flaky roti bread, but then stuffed it with spicy chicken and potato omelette/omelet. I set out to make a vegetarian version of this dish as soon as I returned home, substituting the meat for oak-smoked tofu, which became a popular dish on The Hungry Gecko menu. For an easy version, I follow Malaysian chef Norman Musa's example, and use spring roll pastry instead of making rotis.

SMOKY TOFU MURTABAK
SPICED CRISPY PANCAKE WITH SMOKY TOFU AND NEW POTATO

1 tablespoon vegetable oil, plus extra for brushing and shallow-frying
1 small onion, finely diced
½ teaspoon each of fennel seeds, garam masala, ground coriander and ground cumin
¼ teaspoon each of ground turmeric and chilli/chili powder
½ large red chilli/chile, finely chopped

½ teaspoon soft brown sugar
½ teaspoon salt
150 g/5 oz. new potatoes, unpeeled and diced
4 spring onions/scallions, sliced
350 g/12½ oz. smoked tofu (oak-smoked is my favourite), crumbled
8 sheets of 30-cm/12-in. spring roll pastry
Simple Sambal (page 33), to serve

SERVES 4

Heat the oil in a heavy-based pan over medium heat and cook the onion for 5 minutes or until soft and translucent. Bruise the fennel seeds with a rolling pin to release the aroma, then add all the dried spices to the onion and cook over medium-low heat for 10 minutes. Add the chilli/chile, cook for 1 minute, then add the sugar and salt.

Put the potatoes in a bowl and add half the spring onions/scallions, the spiced onion mixture and the tofu, then mix together well.

Put a spring roll pastry sheet on the work surface and put one-eighth of the mixture in the lower middle section. Fold up the bottom edge of the pastry, then fold in the sides and top to make a thick rectangle – keep the shape even by patting the sides of the pastry. Brush a little oil on the last edge and fold tightly. Ensure there are no gaps at the corners.

Heat the oil for shallow-frying in a frying pan/skillet, then fry each parcel on both sides until crispy and golden. Drain on paper towels. Slice each parcel in half at an angle, sprinkle with the remaining spring onions/scallions and serve with chilli sambal.

PICKLED CUCUMBER SALAD

This super-quick salad brings a little pickled zing to lots of South-east Asian dishes. It is served as an accompaniment with Nasi Lemak (page 168).

1 large cucumber, halved lengthways and deseeded
1 small red chilli/chili, finely chopped
2 tablespoons rice vinegar

1–2 tablespoons caster/superfine sugar
freshly squeezed juice of 1 lime

SERVES 2–4

Slice the cucumber into thin half moons. Mix the remaining ingredients together in a bowl, and stir well until the sugar dissolves. Taste and add more sugar if it's too sour or spicy. Stir in the cucumber and leave to stand for 10–20 minutes before serving.

NASI LEMAK
COCONUT RICE WITH TEMPEH AND MACADAMIA SAMBAL

You will see this hugely popular dish on every Malaysian menu. Traditionally, it was the meal for a big and hearty Malaysian breakfast, often served with anchovies and eggs, but now it's eaten at all times of day (not unlike the British all-day breakfast). Nasi lemak simply means 'creamy or rich rice', which refers to cooking it in coconut milk with pandan leaves. The leaves have a savoury–sweet hint of vanilla. Using smoky tempeh and macadamia nuts creates a protein-rich but deeply flavoured vegan sambal.

3 pandan leaves
400 g/2¼ cups jasmine rice
400 ml/1¾ cups coconut milk
1 teaspoon salt

PASTE
5 large dried red chillies/chiles
100 ml/scant ½ cup vegetable oil
2 small red onions, roughly chopped
2 large red chillies/chiles, finely chopped
4-cm/1½-in. piece of galangal, peeled and finely chopped, or 1 teaspoon ground galangal
2 tablespoons vegan fish sauce (page 13), or light soy sauce and a pinch of seaweed flakes
8–10 macadamia nuts

TEMPEH SAMBAL
1 tablespoon vegetable or groundnut/peanut oil
2 small red onions, finely chopped
100 g/3¾ oz. smoked tempeh, roughly chopped
2 tablespoons vegan fish sauce (page 13), or tamari
65 g/scant ⅓ cup soft brown sugar
1 tablespoon tamarind pulp or paste, or ½ teaspoon tamarind concentrate mixed with a little water
1 teaspoon salt

ACCOMPANIMENTS
500 ml/2 cups vegetable oil, for frying
1 banana shallot, sliced into rings
2–3 tablespoons peanuts
3–4 banana leaves or 12 pandan leaves, to serve (optional)
Pickled Cucumber Salad (page 167), to serve
lime wedges, to serve

SERVES 3–4

Tie the pandan leaves together in a knot and put them in a rice steamer with the rice, coconut milk, 200 ml/scant 1 cup water, and the salt. Mix well, then cook according to the manufacturer's instructions. (Alternatively, bring to the boil in a pan and simmer for 8 minutes or until the rice is almost cooked, then remove the pan from the heat. Cover the pan with a clean dishtowel and replace the lid. Leave to stand for 10–12 minutes. Once cooked, remove the leaves and fluff up the rice with a fork. Cover and set aside.

For the paste, put the dried chillies/chiles in a bowl, cover with hot water and let soak for 10–12 minutes. Drain. Put all the paste ingredients in a food processor or blender and blend to a smooth paste.

To make the sambal, heat the oil in a wok, and fry the paste gently until the oil starts to separate. Add the red onions and cook until they start to soften, then add the remaining sambal ingredients and mix well. Cook gently for 20 minutes.

For the accompaniments, heat the oil in a wok or pan over medium heat. Add the shallot rings and fry until crispy and brown, then remove and drain on paper towels. Toast the peanuts in a dry pan over medium heat for 1–2 minutes, stirring, until golden.

To serve, line each plate with a banana leaf or pandan leaves, if using. Scoop the rice into an individual portion-sized dome-shaped bowl and press down, then turn it out onto the leaves. Repeat with the other servings. Place a large spoonful of the sambal to one side of the rice. Add a small scoop of peanuts and a scoop of pickled cucumber to the other side. Finish with the crispy shallot rings on top. Serve with lime wedges.

RENDANG WITH GREEN JACKFRUIT
JACKFRUIT CURRY WITH COCONUT, LEMONGRASS AND CHILLI/CHILE

Whether rendang is the national dish of Malaysia or Indonesia I'm really not sure. It seems to depend on who you speak to. Either way, it's a celebrated dish that is often eaten as part of wedding celebrations – I used to see this curry (usually beef or sometimes chicken) on many tourist restaurant menus. I never once saw a vegetarian version. Jackfruit is the biggest tree fruit in the world. When it's ripe, it tastes like a cross between an earthy pineapple with a touch of mango. It can also be eaten as a vegetable when it's still green.

10–12 large dried red chillies/chiles, to taste
6 bird's eye or Thai red chillies/chiles, trimmed
1 onion, roughly chopped
6–8 garlic cloves, roughly chopped
6-cm/2½-in. piece of root ginger, peeled and roughly chopped
6-cm/2½-in. piece of galangal, peeled and roughly chopped
4 lemongrass stalks
½ teaspoon ground turmeric, or a 3-cm/1¼-in. piece of fresh turmeric, peeled
2 tablespoons vegetable oil
2 x 400-g/14-oz. cans coconut cream
560 g/20 oz. canned green jackfruit, cut into bite-sized pieces along the fibres

1–2 tablespoons tamarind paste, to taste
1–2 tablespoons soft brown sugar, to taste
4 lime leaves
sea salt
steamed basmati rice, to serve
Pickled Cucumber Salad (page 167), to serve

KERISIK
100 g/3½ oz. creamed coconut (½ block), or 100 g/3½ oz. dessicated/dry unsweetened shredded coconut

CRISPY SHALLOTS
about 500 ml/2 cups vegetable oil
300 g/11 oz. banana shallots, finely chopped

SERVES 4–6

Put the dried chillies/chiles in a bowl and cover with hot water. Leave to soak for 20–30 minutes. Drain.

Put the fresh chillies/chiles in a food processor or blender and add the onion, garlic, ginger, galangal, lemongrass, turmeric and the soaked chillies/chiles, then blend to make a paste.

Heat the oil in a large pan and cook the paste for 5 minutes. Add the coconut cream and 500 ml/2 cups water, and bring to the boil. Add the jackfruit, then bring back to the boil and add the tamarind and brown sugar. Cook for 1–2 hours over low heat until the jackfruit is tender and falling apart a little.

Meanwhile, make the kerisik. Put the creamed coconut in a microwave-proof bowl. Microwave on full power, stirring every few minutes, for 10 minutes until dark brown. Be careful, as it reaches a very high temperature as it browns. If you do not have a microwave or can't find creamed coconut, soak the dessicated/dried unsweetened shredded coconut in boiling water for 15 minutes, then drain and place on a baking sheet. Bake at 190°C (375°F) Gas 5 for 15–20 minutes, moving occasionally, until browned. Blend to a paste using a mortar and pestle.

For the shallots, heat the vegetable oil in a frying pan/skillet over medium-high heat. Add a slice of shallot to the oil. If it sizzles and rises to the surface, the oil is hot enough. Add the sliced shallots and fry until dark golden brown. Remove the shallots with a slotted spoon and drain on paper towels.

Once the jackfruit is tender, add the lime leaves, salt to taste and the kerisik. Serve with rice, crispy shallots on top, and pickled cucumber on the side.

MALAYSIAN STEAMBOAT
STEAMING VEGETABLE HOTPOT

This is a truly social dining dish, not dissimilar to the experience of a Swiss-style fondue. We'd been trekking in the Cameron highlands for a much longer day than we intended because we got a bit lost trying to climb up Gunung Berenbun to get a great view of the surrounding forests and tea plantations. Fortunately, we made it back to our car just before dusk, making a note to ourselves to take a better map next time. We headed back to Tanah Rata, our base town for the week and, after a quick change, our trekking-fuelled hunger led us to a Chinese-Malay café serving vegetarian steamboats with an array of sauces and dips on the side.

A steamboat is simply a pot, traditionally with a charcoal centre, containing boiling broth, which is served at the dining table. Diners dip raw vegetables, seafood and meat into the broth compartments. The array of sauces and dips means everyone adjusts their plate of food to suit their palate. You can easily use a fondue set as a substitute, or put a crockpot on a hotplate or simple burner.

150 g/5 oz. seitan (mock chicken or duck made from gluten), washed and drained

6 tablespoons hoisin sauce

300 g/11 oz. firm tofu, drained and cut into bite-sized pieces

6 tablespoons black bean sauce

2 tablespoons ginger paste, or 7.5-cm/3-in. piece of root ginger, peeled and finely chopped

1 tablespoon toasted sesame oil

1 carrot, quartered lengthways and cut into 4 cm/1½ in. sticks

1 courgette/zucchini, quartered lengthways and cut into 4 cm/ 1½ in. sticks

8 chestnut mushrooms, halved

120 g/4 oz. enoki mushrooms, trimmed

120 g/4 oz. oyster mushrooms, torn into bite-sized pieces

100 g/3¾ oz. mangetouts/ snow peas

1 pak choi/bok choy

a large handful of beansprouts

1 spring onion/scallion, thinly sliced

240 ml/1 cup light soy sauce

½ teaspoon sesame seeds

1 tablespoon Simple Sambal (page 33)

freshly squeezed juice of 2 limes

350 g/12 oz. vermicelli rice noodles

BROTH

4 dried shiitake mushrooms, stalks snipped off

freshly squeezed juice of 2 limes

4 garlic cloves, crushed

100 ml/scant ½ cup sake

2 lemongrass stalks, heavily bruised

½ teaspoon salt, or to taste

2 tablespoons light soy sauce or tamari

steamboat or crockpot
3 baking sheets, greased

SERVES 4

Page 172–173: Malaysian Steamboat.

Put all the broth ingredients and 2 litres/quarts water in a large pan and bring to the boil, then reduce the heat and simmer for about 30–40 minutes. Check the seasoning and add a little more salt if needed. Preheat the oven to 180°C (350°F) Gas 4.

Tear the seitan into smaller pieces and put in a shallow bowl. Add 2 tablespoons of the hoisin sauce, then set aside for 10 minutes. Put half the tofu pieces in another bowl and add 2 tablespoons of the black bean sauce. Put all the remaining tofu in a third bowl and add the ginger and sesame oil. Leave the bowls for 10 minutes for the ingredients to marinate.

Spread the marinated seitan and tofu onto the prepared baking sheets. Put all the baking sheets in the oven and cook for about 20–25 minutes until the edges are starting to crisp. Cool on the baking sheets, then put the seitan and tofu on a large serving plate. Put the vegetables, except the spring onion/scallion, into small serving bowls ready for dipping and cooking at the table.

Put 120 ml/½ cup of the soy sauce in a bowl and add the spring onion/scallion and sesame seeds. Fill several small dipping pots with the simple sambal, lime juice and the remaining hoisin and black bean sauces, ready for the table. Soak the noodles in boiling water for 10 minutes, then drain in a colander and transfer to a serving bowl.

To serve, heat the steamboat or crockpot, then add the broth. Bring to the boil, then reduce to a simmer. Lay the bowls and plates around the steamboat. Each person should have their own small bowl and chopsticks. They take it in turns to drop vegetables, seitan, and tofu into the broth, along with a few noodles, cook them for a few minutes then ladle them into their own bowl. The diner can then add sauces, dips and lime juice to their own taste. Each diner usually has three or four different bowlfuls over the course of the evening.

BAKED SPRING ROLLS
CRISPY STUFFED ROLLS WITH GINGER, SESAME AND HOLY BASIL

Spring rolls are an undisputable crowd pleaser, but they can have a tendency to be greasy, and if you buy them ready-made, the filling is often an indistinguishable mush. These rolls are simple to make, and a tad healthier than the deep-fried version. They can easily be frozen, once prepared and rolled, then cooked as required. I play around with the fillings, and the hoisin seitan filling (page 157) works well, mixed with noodles, spring onions/scallions and sesame oil for a delicious vegan take on a crispy duck spring roll.

100 g/3½ oz. vermicelli rice noodles

4–5-cm/1½–2-in. piece of root ginger, peeled and finely chopped

a large handful of fresh holy basil, or a mixture of mint and European basil, chopped, plus extra leaves to garnish

1 small red chilli/chile, deseeded and finely chopped

100 g/3½ oz. water chestnuts, diced

100 g/3½ oz. bamboo shoots, roughly chopped

8 baby sweetcorn/corn, sliced

80 g/1½ cups beansprouts

2 tablespoons toasted sesame oil, plus extra if needed and to brush

8 sheets of 30-cm/12-in. spring roll wrapper

SOY DIP

6 tablespoons light soy sauce

1 spring onion/scallion, thinly sliced

¼ teaspoon sesame seeds

1 small red chilli/chile, deseeded and finely chopped

baking sheet, greased

MAKES 8

Soak the noodles in boiling water for 10 minutes, then drain in a sieve/strainer. Put the noodles in a large bowl and, using sharp scissors, snip at the noodles to make shortened and more manageable strands. Add all the remaining ingredients, except the spring roll wrappers, to the bowl and mix well, adding more sesame oil if needed to ensure everything is well mixed and the vegetables and flavours are evenly dispersed.

Preheat the oven to 180°C (350°F) Gas 4.

Lay a sheet of spring roll wrapper on the work surface (keep the remaining wrappers covered with a damp dish towel), and brush the edges with sesame oil. Put some filling 6 cm/2½ in. above the bottom edge in a line but not all the way to each side. Leave at least a 4-cm/1½-in. space at each end.

Lift the edge closest to you and tuck it under the filling. Roll quite tightly, so that the filling is snug. Push in any filling that may be spilling out at each end, then fold each side in, to create neat and firmly folded ends. Roll again, tucking snugly as you go, to the end of the pastry, and brush lightly with oil to ensure the edges are well sealed. Put on the prepared baking sheet leaving enough space in between so that they will cook evenly. Repeat until all the rolls are filled. Bake for 20–30 minutes until golden brown and crispy, turning once.

To make the dip, put the soy sauce in a small serving bowl and add the spring onion/scallion, sesame seeds and red chilli/chile. Serve the spring rolls immediately with the soy dip. Garnish with some holy basil leaves.

SWEET-&-SOUR POPCORN TOFU
FIVE-SPICE PANKO-FRIED TOFU WITH PLUM SWEET-&-SOUR SAUCE

This is another fusion-style dish that I created as an appetizer for a dining event. In my quest to give tofu texture and flavour, there are quite a lot of processes involved, but you can save time by using a ready-made plum sauce, if you like. For an impressive appetizer, put a little sauce in a Chinese soup spoon and top with a piece of tofu. You can also serve these as a main course with steamed rice.

6 tablespoons light soy sauce

2 teaspoons Chinese five-spice powder

400 g/14 oz. firm tofu, cut into bite-sized pieces

150 g/1 cups cornflour/cornstarch

100 ml/⅓ cup soya/soy cream

150 g/2¾ cups panko breadcrumbs

1 teaspoon hot smoked paprika

vegetable oil, for deep-frying

steamed rice (optional), to serve

PLUM SAUCE

12 plums, stoned/pitted and roughly chopped

4–6 tablespoons soft brown sugar, if using plums

8 tablespoons rice vinegar, or to taste

1 tablespoon tomato purée/paste, or to taste

½ teaspoon salt

SERVES 4–6

To make the sauce, put the plums in a pan over medium heat and add 2 tablespoons water and the sugar. Bring to the boil, then simmer for 15 minutes or until the fruit is completely softened. Add the remaining sauce ingredients and bring to a simmer again, adding a little water if necessary so that the sauce is not too thick. Using a food processor or blender, blend the sauce until smooth. Check the seasoning and adjust the sugar, salt or vinegar to taste. The balance of sweet-and-sour flavours means one should not overpower the other.

Mix the soy sauce and five-spice powder in a small bowl, then drizzle this marinade over the tofu pieces. Put the cornflour/cornstarch in one bowl, the soya/soy cream in another bowl and the panko breadcrumbs in a third bowl. Add the paprika to the panko breadcrumbs and mix well.

Heat 600 ml/2½ cups vegetable oil in a wok over medium–high heat. Put a sheet of greaseproof paper on the work surface. Dip each piece of tofu in the cornflour/cornstarch, then in the soya/soy cream and then in the breadcrumbs, shaping it a little to form a ball. Lay each coated ball on the greaseproof paper as you go.

Fry the tofu balls in batches, until golden brown and crispy. Lift out using a slotted spoon and drain on paper towels. You can keep the tofu balls warm in a low oven at 140°C (275°F) Gas 1, if you like, or reheat them later at 170°C (350°F) Gas 4 for 10–15 minutes. Serve with the plum sauce.

Indonesia

Lee and I travelled to Indonesia when we first met in the early nineties. We had never been to Asia before, so instead of gently introducing ourselves, we flew into Bangkok and jumped straight on a train down to Butterworth in Malaysia, before hopping on a boat to Medan, the capital of North Sumatra. We spent 2 hours in Medan bus station trying to figure out which bus would take us to Lake Toba, a beautiful crater lake. We eventually set off the next day (with a chicken on my lap) but after six hours, and as the last people on the bus, we were unceremoniously dumped in the middle of nowhere and told that the bus stopped here. We did eventually find our way to the lake and Samosir Island, and it was even more breathtaking than we could have imagined.

The biggest food revelation for me in Indonesia was discovering I liked tempeh (tempe). I had tried it before at home, but never really taken to it. Tempeh is a fermented cake of soya/soy beans, where unlike tofu, the bean is whole, so there's a lot of texture and bite. Tempeh makes the best bacon substitute for vegans, by simply slicing and frying it in a little soy sauce. Stick it in a doorstop sandwich with some lettuce and tomato, and you'll be in vegan sandwich heaven. Because it's already fermented, it's very stable without refrigeration (although I do suggest you keep it in the fridge). It's easy to make too (but I prefer to buy it), so it's an essential protein source for Indonesians across the

archipelago. They snack on it street-side, they make curries with it, and they dip it in all manner of delicious sauces. During MasterChef, I served some Balinese-style satay skewers made with tempeh, which John Torode thought was a "very clever vegan dish".

We've returned to Indonesia twice as a family since that first trip, and it still feels wildly unexplored each time. We became quite skilled free-divers around the islands and coasts of this stunning archipelago, with its crystal blue coral-filled water and smoky-topped volcanoes. It was easy to lose yourself for hours following a turtle or two, or trying not to breathe too heavily as a white tip shark passes by under the dark shadows of the reef shelf. We cooked our breakfast on the side of a volcano, travelled for days to reach remote islands and often felt like we were in the middle of filming a David Attenborough documentary, with the prolific and diverse wildlife there. I've often day dreamed about opening a café on a hillside in Lombok, such is my love for the place. I could live there for a while I think, just so I could spend a bit of each day underwater.

From left to right: Forest statue, Bali; Fishing boats on beach, Lombok; Dawn across Nusa Tengarra; Public bus, northern Lombok; Komodo National Park; Cooking bananas in volcano, Gunung Batur, Bali; Gunung Rinjani sunset, Lombok.

GADO-GADO

INDONESIAN VEGETABLE SALAD AND SPICY PEANUT SAUCE

This was the very first dish I ate in Indonesia. We were in Medan for the night and both feeling a tad bewildered. I had heard of gado-gado before, so when I spotted the sign outside a main street café, we headed inside in the hope of something not too unfamiliar to eat. The tempeh was the biggest surprise, having been crisply fried in soy sauce, it tasted unlike any I had sampled at home. The peanut sauce was sweet, sticky and spicy, and I soon learned this was a staple among many Indonesian dishes. You can also serve it with Ginger-baked Tofu (page 198) and Lontong (page 194).

150 g/1 cup small new potatoes, quartered
2 large carrots, cut into sticks
150 g/5 oz. fine green beans, cut into 4-cm/1½-in. lengths
75 g/1 cup cauliflower florets
350 g/12 oz. tempeh or firm tofu, cut into 1-cm/½-in. slices
2 tablespoons light soy sauce or tamari
2 tablespoons vegetable oil, plus extra for shallow-frying
1 small red onion, thinly sliced (optional)
½ cucumber, halved lengthways
60 g/1 cup beansprouts

GADO-GADO SAUCE (SAMBAL KACANG)
300 g/2¼ cups roasted peanuts or crunchy peanut butter
2 garlic cloves, crushed
400 ml/1¾ cups coconut milk
1 tablespoon dried red chilli flakes/hot pepper flakes, or 1 teaspoon hot chilli/chili powder
1 teaspoon garam masala
7.5-cm/3-in. piece of fresh turmeric, peeled, or ½ teaspoon ground turmeric
1–2 teaspoons soft brown sugar, to taste (omit if using peanut butter)
1 tablespoon dark soy sauce
2 tablespoons tamarind water, or lime or lemon juice
½ teaspoon salt, or to taste

SERVES 4–6

Boil the potatoes in water to cover for 8 minutes or until tender, then drain. Boil a separate large pan of water. Plunge the carrots, green beans and cauliflower in the water and blanch for 2 minutes, then drain in a colander and set aside to cool.

Marinate the tempeh or tofu in the soy sauce for 5 minutes. Heat the oil in a frying pan/skillet over medium–high heat and fry the tempeh until golden. Drain on paper towels.

If using the red onion, heat oil for shallow-frying in the frying pan/skillet over medium–high heat and fry the onion slices until they are crispy and golden. Drain on paper towels. Using a teaspoon, scrape out the watery seeds from the centre of the cucumber. Slice the flesh into sticks and set aside.

To make the gado-gado sauce, put the peanuts in a food processor or blender and add the garlic, half the coconut milk, the chilli flakes/hot pepper flakes, garam masala, turmeric and sugar (omit if using peanut butter) and blend until smooth.

Put the mixture in a small pan over medium-low heat and combine with the remaining coconut milk, the dark soy sauce and tamarind water, then heat gently, stirring occasionally. Simmer gently for 7 minutes. Add a little salt to taste, and more sugar or chilli flakes/hot pepper flakes if needed. It should be sweet and spicy with a savoury depth.

To serve, put the vegetables, cucumber, beansprouts and tempeh onto a serving plate, and pour over some of the warm peanut sauce. Garnish with the crispy fried onions, if using. The peanut sauce will keep for up to 1 week in the fridge.

TAHU BAKAR
CRISPY STUFFED TOFU POCKETS

This popular snack from Indonesia is also found in Malaysia. Kecap manis is an Indonesian sweet soy sauce that is flavoured with garlic and sometimes star anise. The tofu should be the fresh firm variety that hasn't been frozen, so as to maintain the soft middle with a crispy outside.

vegetable oil, for deep-frying

800 g/1¾ lb. firm tofu, cut into 8 squares, 6 cm/2½ in across

1 large cucumber, halved lengthways

100 g/1¾ cups beansprouts

3 tablespoons peanuts

SAUCE

2 tablespoons soft brown sugar

1–2 small red chillies/chiles, finely chopped

2 tablespoons tamarind water, or 1 teaspoon tamarind concentrate dissolved in 2 tablespoons hot water

1 tablespoon vegan fish sauce (page 13), or light soy sauce and a pinch of seaweed flakes

3 tablespoons kecap manis (Indonesian sweet soy sauce)

SERVES 4–6

Put all the sauce ingredients in a food processor or blender and process to make a thick sauce.

Heat the oil in a wok or large pan and deep-fry the tofu pieces in batches for 2–3 minutes until they are golden brown and crispy on the outside. Drain on paper towels and set aside to cool.

Using a teaspoon, scrape out the seeds from the centre of the cucumber. Slice the flesh thinly at an angle. Bring a large pan of water to the boil. Add the beansprouts and blanch for 30 seconds. Drain, then set aside on paper towels. Toast the peanuts in a dry pan over medium heat for 1–2 minutes, stirring occasionally, until golden. Chop them, then set aside.

Preheat the grill/broiler. Cut a slit horizontally into the tofu pieces to make a pocket. Brush a little sauce onto the outside. Grill/broil for 3 minutes on each side. Drizzle a little marinade inside the tofu pocket, then stuff some beansprouts and cucumber pieces inside, with some sticking out. Drizzle with more sauce, then scatter toasted peanuts on top.

SINGKONG GORENG
SPICED CASSAVA CHIPS

My husband tells me that they serve some very good coffee in Indonesia. I'm a tea drinker, so I leave that evaluation to him. What I didn't mind poaching from him were some of the cassava chips they often serve with good coffee. You can dip these in a simple sambal or serve them as part of an Indonesian dinner. It's easy to find cassava as it's popular in Asia and Africa, so local Afro-Caribbean or Asian grocery shops always stock it, as do many major supermarkets in the UK and US.

½ tablespoon ground coriander

3 garlic cloves, crushed

¼ teaspoon ground turmeric

½ teaspoon salt, to taste

500 g/1 lb. 2 oz. cassava, peeled and cut into 5-cm/2-in. pieces and then into chips/fries

vegetable oil, for shallow-frying

SERVES 3–4

Preheat the oven to 110°C (225°F) Gas ¼ and put a baking sheet in to warm.

Toast the coriander in a dry pan over medium heat for 30 seconds, stirring occasionally, to release the aroma. Put the garlic in a large bowl and add the coriander, turmeric and salt, then mix well.

Boil the cassava pieces in water to cover for 10–15 minutes until just soft. Drain on paper towels. While still warm, add the cassava to the spice mix in the bowl. Coat well and leave to marinate for 15 minutes.

Heat the oil in a wok over medium-high heat. Fry the cassava pieces in batches for 10 minutes or until golden brown, turning occasionally. Lift out with a slotted spoon and drain on paper towels; place back on the baking sheet and keep warm in the oven while you cook the remaining cassava. Serve immediately.

BULUNG KUAH PINDANG
BALI-STYLE SEAWEED SALAD

We often came across versions of this salad (sans shrimp paste or kuah pindang) around the cafés of tranquil Ubud and the less-than-tranquil Kuta beach. The Lonely Planet describes Ubud as a place 'where all that is magical about Bali comes together in one easy-to-love package'. I'd say that's about right, although I would also recommend climbing one of Bali's volcanoes for sunrise if you really want to experience something magical. My mum had come out to visit us for two weeks, which made it all the more special. Sitting atop Gunung Batur with my mum (after a three-hour pre-dawn climb), we watched the children excitedly bake bananas in the ground, while we watched the sun break through from behind neighbouring Gunung Rinjani. Mum said it was one of the best moments of her life.

My version of this salad includes local ingredients and seeds for a nutrient-packed salad, with the addition of some rather European croûtons. You can use whatever seaweed you can source and adapt the level of spice for a more family-friendly recipe too.

2 slices of bread, crusts removed and cut into 1-cm/½-in. squares
sesame oil, to drizzle
50 g/2 oz. curly kale, stalks removed, torn into 4-cm/1½-in. pieces
2 tablespoons groundnut/peanut oil
200-g/7-oz. can red kidney beans, rinsed and drained
1 teaspoon each of sesame and pumpkin seeds (optional)
10 g/⅓ oz. laver, soaked in cold water, rinsed and sliced
10 g/⅓ oz. dulse, soaked in cold water, rinsed and sliced
10 g/⅓ oz. arame, soaked in cold water and rinsed
10 g/⅓ oz. wakame, soaked in cold water and rinsed

4 radishes, cut into matchsticks
2–3 spring onions/scallions, thinly sliced diagonally
salt and white pepper

SAMBAL DRESSING
1 large green banana, peeled
2 tablespoons light soy sauce or tamari
½ teaspoon sesame oil
1 tablespoon vegan fish sauce (page 13), or light soy sauce and a pinch of seaweed flakes
½ tablespoon soft brown sugar, or to taste
1–4 bird's eye chillies/chiles, finely chopped
2 tablespoons desiccated/dry unsweetened shredded coconut

SERVES 4–6

Preheat the oven to 120°C (250°F) Gas ½.

Put the bread cubes on a baking sheet and drizzle with sesame oil. Bake for 15–20 minutes until crispy and just browned. Set aside to cool.

To make the dressing, put the green banana in a food processor or blender and add the soy sauce, sesame oil, vegan fish sauce, sugar and chillies/chiles. (You can add 1 chilli/chile at a time to see how hot you want the dressing to become. The sweetness of the green banana will counter the heat in the chilli, which is then balanced against the salty seaweed.) Add a little more sugar if there is not enough sweetness from the banana.

Bring a small pan of water to the boil and cook the kale leaves for 1–2 minutes until just tender, then drain on paper towels and cool. Heat the groundnut/peanut oil in a small frying pan/skillet and fry the kidney beans for 5 minutes, tossing gently. Drain on paper towels.

Toast the sesame seeds and pumpkin seeds, if using, in a dry pan over medium heat for about 1–2 minutes, stirring occasionally, until golden. Toast the coconut for the dressing in a second pan.

Put the laver, dulse, arame and wakame in a bowl and add the radish sticks, spring onions/scallions, kale and toasted seeds. Mix together, then stir the coconut into the sambal dressing, and mix well into the salad. Just before serving, add the sesame croutons and season with salt and pepper, to taste. Mix well. To serve, heap the mixture into a large serving bowl. Scatter the fried kidney beans on top of the salad to finish.

From left to right: Bulung Kuah Pindang; Tahu Bakar sauce; Singkong Goreng; Tahu Bakar.

TEMPE BACEM
TWICE-COOKED TEMPEH

When we returned to Indonesia with the children, we spent most of our time travelling from Bali down the Nusa Tengarra, the string of islands to the east, ending up in Flores. After Bali, our next stop was Lombok, and I fell in love with the island immediately. Bali is beautiful and quite spiritual, there is no doubt about that. Lombok is its more rugged and less-developed neighbour, with pristine reefs and some of the best free-diving I've ever experienced. If you want to swim with turtles, sun fish and manta rays, get yourself over to Lombok's Gili islands, if you ever get the chance.

I ate this snack for the first time while waiting for a boat in Mataram's port, Lombok's capital. I was wandering around town looking for somewhere to buy a new pair of flip-flops when I saw some school children filling their pockets with little bags of this snack from a street vendor. It formed part of another great boat picnic.

1 small onion, finely chopped
2 garlic cloves, finely chopped
1 teaspoon ground coriander
1-cm/½-in. piece of root ginger, peeled and grated, or 1 teaspoon ginger paste
1 bay leaf
1-cm/½-in. piece of fresh galangal, peeled and chopped, or ½ teaspoon ground galangal
1 generous teaspoon soft brown sugar (optional)
½ teaspoon chilli/chili powder
1 teaspoon tamarind concentrate, dissolved in 250 ml/1 cup warm water
350 g/12 oz. tempeh, cut into 1 cm/½ in. thick bite-sized slices
1–2 tablespoons groundnut/peanut or vegetable oil

SERVES 3–4

Put all the ingredients, except the tempeh and the oil, into a medium pan and bring to the boil, then reduce the heat to a simmer.

Add the tempeh to the pan. Add water to cover and cook gently for 40 minutes or until all the liquid has been absorbed by the tempeh. Keep a close eye as the liquid is absorbed so that the tempeh doesn't burn. Set aside and leave to cool.

Heat the oil in a heavy-based frying pan/skillet. Add the slices of tempeh and fry until golden and starting to crisp, about 3–4 minutes on each side. Drain on paper towels and cool. Serve warm or cold. These can be stored in an air-tight container in the fridge for up to a week.

TAHU CAMPUR
JAVANESE FRIED TOFU WITH CASSAVA CAKES

We never got to explore Java. From Sumatra across the archipelago to Flores we've visited most of the main islands (although Sulawesi is also on the 'still to explore' list). But like lots of the countries we have visited, we tended to spend a longer time in places than your average young backpacker. This means there are a lot of places on the traveller's trail we missed, often because places are just so vast and with so much to see. With seven-year-old twins in tow, we travelled at a slower pace with no mind for traveller tick lists. But there's still plenty of time to return, I hope. I often dream and scheme of just how we could reach the remote Maluku islands. Apparently, it's like the Maldives before the airports were built and the money arrived. Hence the challenge in getting there!

This dish had to be included because it's a classic Indonesian street food dish, and it is often vegan since using beef is expensive and hard to come by in more remote places. The cassava cakes are a lovely vegan addition, and to my mind they make the dish complete without meat. The dish originates from East Java, the world's most populous island, so it's no wonder the dish has travelled and been adapted across the archipelago. We tried this dish in Flores, and the cheekily hidden spice of sambal at the bottom of the bowl was a surprise. I like to serve it on the side as well, for some extra spicy dipping. I use a Korean fermented soya/soy bean paste instead of a beef broth in my recipe. You can serve it with steamed rice, but noodles are more traditional.

350 g/12 oz. firm tofu, rinsed and drained, cut into 5-cm/2-in. cubes, or use deep-fried tofu puffs
2 banana shallots, sliced into rings
350-g/12-oz. packet of egg-free yellow noodles
100 g/1¾ cups beansprouts
vegetable oil, for deep-frying
Cassava Cakes (page 192), to serve

BROTH
6 candlenuts, boiled vigorously for 10–15 minutes, or macadamia nuts
1 teaspoon ground coriander
5-cm/2-in. piece of galangal, peeled, or 1 teaspoon ground galangal
2 lemongrass stalks
5 kaffir lime leaves
2 bay leaves
1 tablespoon kecap manis (Indonesian sweet soy sauce)
1 tablespoon soft brown sugar
5-cm/2-in. piece of root ginger, peeled and roughly chopped
5-cm/2-in. piece of fresh turmeric, peeled and roughly chopped, or ½ teaspoon ground turmeric
15 black peppercorns
2 small red onions, roughly chopped
2 tablespoons fermented soya/soy bean paste
5 garlic cloves, peeled
1 large red chilli/chile
1 tablespoon tamarind pulp or paste, or ¼ teaspoon tamarind concentrate
1 litre/quart vegetable stock
1 tablespoon vegetable oil

SAMBAL
vegetable oil, for shallow-frying
8 garlic cloves, thinly sliced
12 red bird's eye chillies/chiles, trimmed
a pinch of salt
½ tablespoon sugar
½ tablespoon dark soy sauce

SERVES 3–4

To make the broth, boil the candlenuts vigorously in water to cover for 15 minutes, then drain. Toast the coriander in a dry pan over medium heat for 30 seconds, stirring occasionally, to release the aroma. Crush the galangal, lemongrass, lime leaves and bay leaves, so that they are well bruised and fractured. Put the candlenuts, coriander all and the remaining ingredients, except the bruised flavourings, stock and oil, in a food processor or blender and process until smooth, using some of the stock to help make a paste.

Heat the vegetable oil in a large pan over high heat, and fry the paste for 2–3 minutes, then add the galangal, lemongrass, lime leaves and bay leaves. Stir-fry for another 1–2 minutes, then add the stock and 1 litre/quart water. Simmer for 40 minutes. Remove the lemongrass, galangal and bay leaves.

Heat the oil for deep-frying in a wok or large, heavy-based pan, then deep-fry the tofu cubes (not the deep-fried tofu puffs) until golden brown. Drain on paper towels and leave to cool. Deep-fry the banana shallots in the same way. Set aside. Cut the tofu cubes, or the tofu puffs, into thick slices. You can use the oil to deep-fry the cassava cakes (opposite) at this stage too.

To make the sambal, heat the oil in a small saucepan over medium-high heat and cook the garlic slices until fried and crisp. Drain on paper towels. Put the garlic and all the remaining ingredients in a food processor or blender and process to make a thick paste. Set aside.

Cook the noodles according to the packet instructions, then drain. To serve, place ¼ teaspoon sambal, or according to taste, in the bottom of each serving bowl. Layer a good mixture of the noodles and beansprouts on top, then add the slices of fried tofu. Ladle over the broth, ensuring everything is well covered, then add 2 cassava cakes, and sprinkle with fried shallots.

CASSAVA CAKES
INDONESIAN-STYLE SAVOURY CAKES

Cassava is used in sweet and savoury cakes on many of the islands. These savoury ones make a great gluten-free snack, and can be served on their own with some spicy sambal or as part of an Indonesian rice table (a banquet of little dishes adapted by the Dutch colonials, known as rijsttafel).

1 teaspoon ground coriander
3 garlic cloves, roughly chopped
80 g/3¼ oz. silken tofu freshly squeezed juice of ½ lime
½ teaspoon mild chilli/chili powder
½ small red onion, roughly chopped

500 g/1 lb. 2 oz. cassava, peeled and coarsely grated
5 chives, finely snipped
1–2 tablespoons rice flour, as needed
½ teaspoon salt, to taste
vegetable oil, for deep-frying

MAKES 8–10

Toast the coriander in a dry pan over medium heat for 30 seconds, stirring occasionally, to release the aroma. Put the garlic in a food processor or blender and add the coriander, tofu, lime juice, chilli/chili powder and onion. Blend to make a smooth paste. Put the cassava and chives in a large bowl and stir in the spice paste. Add a little rice flour to help bind the mixture, if needed. Season with the salt.

Heat the oil for deep-frying in a wok or large, heavy-based pan, then spoon small (golf ball-sized) balls of the cassava mixture into the hot oil. Fry in batches for 8–10 minutes until golden brown. Remove with a slotted spoon and drain on paper towels. Serve.

BALINESE-STYLE SATAY SKEWERS
FRAGRANT SKEWERS WITH TEMPEH AND TOFU

I served this dish during the fine-dining challenge on MasterChef, where I set out to create a dining experience from a classic street food dish (satay skewers). Compressed rice sticks (lontong) are popular throughout Indonesia, Malaysia and Singapore, and are served alongside all manner of dishes from soups and broths to curries and dipping sauces. They are easy to make with a little patience and can be cut into angular shapes to look attractive.

3 tablespoons desiccated/dry unsweetened shredded coconut

400 ml/1¾ cups coconut milk

2 banana shallots, roughly chopped

3 garlic cloves, roughly chopped

4–5-cm/1½–2-in. piece of root ginger, peeled and roughly chopped

1 teaspoon white pepper

freshly squeezed juice of 1 lime

½ teaspoon salt, plus extra to taste

350 g/12 oz. smoked tempeh, crumbled

100 g/3¾ oz. firm tofu, crumbled

2 tablespoons rice flour, plus extra if needed

8 lemongrass stalks

Lontong (page 194), Chilli Cashews (page 194) and fresh coriander cilantro, to serve

**PEANUT SAUCE
(SAMBAL KACANG)**

300 g/2¼ cups peanuts or crunchy peanut butter

2 garlic cloves, crushed

7.5-cm/3-in. piece of fresh turmeric, peeled, or ½ teaspoon ground turmeric

3 shallots or 1 small red onion, chopped

½ teaspoon salt

1–2 teaspoons soft brown sugar (omit if using peanut butter)

400 ml/1¾ cups coconut milk

1 tablespoon dried red chilli flakes/hot pepper flakes, or 1 teaspoon chilli/chili powder

1 teaspoon garam masala

1–2 tablespoons vegetable oil, for frying

1 tablespoon dark soy sauce

2 tablespoons tamarind water or lime/lemon juice

100 ml/scant ½ cup coconut oil

SERVES 4

Put the desiccated/dry unsweetened shredded coconut in a small bowl and add hot water to cover. Leave to soak for 15–20 minutes. Drain and squeeze out the excess water. Set aside. Put the coconut milk in a food processor or blender and add the shallots, garlic, ginger, white pepper, lime juice and salt. Blend until smooth, then transfer the mixture to a large bowl.

Add the tempeh, tofu and rehydrated coconut to the bowl. Add the rice flour and mix to make a firm, shapeable mixture – add more flour if needed. Divide the mixture into 16 small balls and transfer to a plate. Chill in the fridge for at least 20 minutes.

Meanwhile, remove the outer layer of the lemongrass stalks and trim the ends to make skewers, then soak them in water for 15 minutes. Slide two balls of the tempeh mixture onto each stick – it's easier to do this by sliding from the thin end to halfway onto the thick part of the stick. Squeeze gently to mould the balls together and evenly cover the stick. Cover the exposed end of the lemongrass skewers with foil to stop them from burning when they are grilled/broiled later.

To make the peanut sauce, toast the peanuts in a dry pan over medium heat for 1–2 minutes, stirring occasionally, until golden. Put the peanuts or peanut butter in a food processor or blender and add the garlic, turmeric, shallots, salt, half the sugar (omit if using peanut butter), the coconut milk, dried chilli flakes/hot pepper flakes and garam masala, then process to make a thick paste.

Heat the 1–2 tablespoons vegetable oil for frying in a frying pan/skillet, add the paste and bring it to a simmer. Cook over medium heat for 6–7 minutes, then add the dark soy sauce and tamarind water. Remove from the heat, stir well and set aside.

Put 120 ml/½ cup water in a medium pan over high heat and bring to the boil, then reduce the heat and gradually whisk in the coconut oil to make an emulsion. Add the spice paste to the pan, whisking together with the coconut emulsion, and simmer for 15 minutes, stirring occasionally and adding more water if the sauce becomes too thick. Add the remaining sugar, or to taste, and reheat gently before serving.

Preheat the grill/broiler. Grill/broil the skewers for 7–10 minutes on each side until golden brown. Serve 2 skewers per person. Put the skewers on a plate, and add the peanut sauce and lontong. Serve with the chilli cashews and fresh coriander/cilantro.

LONTONG
COMPRESSED RICE STICKS

200 g/heaped 1 cup
   Thai jasmine rice
½–1 teaspoon salt
2 sticks of cassia
   bark/cinnamon

3 bay leaves
2 black cardamom pods

SERVES 4

Put 1 litre/quart boiling water in a large pan over high heat and add the rice. Add the salt to taste, the cassia bark/cinnamon, bay leaves and cardamom. Bring to the boil and simmer for 10 minutes, then remove the pan from the heat, cover tightly and leave to rest for 10 minutes. Drain the cooked rice in a colander ensuring as much water as possible is removed. Discard the flavourings.

Line a 4 cm/1½ in. deep roasting pan with clingfilm/plastic wrap and fill it with the cooked rice. Press down firmly and cover with more clingfilm/plastic wrap. Put a second roasting pan on top of the rice, press it firmly and weight it down with weights or heavy cans. Transfer to the fridge for 20 minutes, or preferably 1 hour, then remove the clingfilm/plastic wrap and use a sharp knife to cut the rice into 5 cm/2 in. fingers or triangles. Serve.

CHILLI CASHEWS
CARAMELIZED SPICY CASHEW NUTS

20–25 cashew nuts,
   unsalted
50 g/¼ cup caster/
   superfine sugar
1 teaspoon liquid glucose
   (optional)

2 tablespoons sesame
   seeds
1–2 teaspoons dried red
   chilli flakes/hot pepper
   flakes

SERVES 4

Preheat the oven to 180°C (350°F) Gas 4.

Spread the cashews over a non-stick baking sheet and roast for 10 minutes, shaking them occasionally to ensure that they cook evenly. Meanwhile, put the sugar and 1 tablespoon water in a small, heavy-based pan over medium heat and heat to make a syrup (you can add the glucose to help prevent crystals forming, if you like) – do not stir. Once the syrup is dark golden brown, coat the cashews in the syrup, then leave to cool slightly. Scatter the sesame seeds and chilli flakes/hot pepper flakes on a sheet of greaseproof paper and roll the cashews in the seeds and chilli flakes/hot pepper flakes so that a smattering sticks to the caramel. Leave the cashews to cool completely.

HUNGRY GECKO JUNGLE CURRY
COUNTRY VEGETABLE CURRY WITH TEMPEH

Every guesthouse or café seems to have its own version of jungle curry in Indonesia and Borneo. Jungle curry simply means country curry, with full-bodied flavours from an uncomplicated recipe. The Thai version from the central and Northern provinces doesn't contain coconut and is fearsomely hot. In Indonesia, it tends to have a sour quality from tamarind, and while not authentic to most jungle curry recipes, it often contains coconut milk, which tempers some of that equally fierce heat. This recipe is from my street food menu. It is a substantial curry that zings with tamarind and lemongrass in a coconut and turmeric-flavoured sauce. In keeping with the jungle curry ethos, it's very quick to prepare.

280 g/10 oz. tempeh, or green jackfruit, cut into bite-sized pieces
2–3 large red dried chillies/chiles
1–2 large red chillies/chiles, roughly chopped
5-cm/2-in. piece of root ginger, peeled and roughly chopped, or 2 tablespoons ginger paste
5-cm/2-in. piece of galangal, peeled and roughly chopped, or 2 tablespoons galangal paste
3 lemongrass stalks, roughly chopped
4-cm/1½-in. piece of turmeric root, or 1 teaspoon ground turmeric
4 tablespoons vegetable oil, plus extra if needed
1 aubergine/eggplant, cut into bite-sized pieces
1 litre/quart vegetable stock

400 ml/1¾ cups coconut milk
4 tablespoons tamarind pulp or paste, or 2 teaspoons tamarind concentrate, dissolved in 4 tablespoons hot water
2 tablespoons soft brown sugar
2 kaffir lime leaves
2 carrots, sliced
150 g/5 oz. green beans, trimmed
1 teaspoon salt, or to taste
1 tablespoon soy sauce, or to taste
fresh coriander/cilantro leaves, to garnish
100 g/heaped ¾ cup chopped, toasted cashew nuts or peanuts, to serve
steamed rice, to serve

baking sheet, greased

SERVES 4

Preheat the oven to 210°C (400°F) Gas 6.

Place the tempeh on the prepared baking sheet and bake for 10–15 minutes until slightly crispy. Drain on paper towels. (You can omit this step, but it gives a nice texture.)

Put the dried chillies/chiles in a bowl and cover with hot water. Leave to soak for 15 minutes. Drain and roughly chop. Put the dried and fresh chillies/chiles in a food processor or blender with the ginger, galangal, lemongrass and turmeric, then process to make a thick paste. Add a little oil if needed, as this will help the lemongrass and galangal (which are both quite tough) blend to a smooth paste.

Heat the oil in a large, heavy-based pan over high heat and add the spice paste. Cook for 3–4 minutes. Add the aubergine/eggplant and fry for 2 minutes. Add the stock and the coconut milk, along with the tamarind, sugar and lime leaves. Bring to the boil, then reduce the heat and simmer for 15–20 minutes until the aubergine is soft. Add the baked tempeh, the carrots and green beans. Season with the salt and soy sauce to taste.

Cook over low heat for 5–7 minutes until the carrots and beans are just cooked – add more water if needed so the sauce is not too thick. Garnish with coriander/cilantro and serve with cashews and rice.

NASI GORENG
INDONESIAN STIR-FRIED RICE WITH GINGER-BAKED TOFU

This is one of the best-selling dishes on my street food menu. It is to Indonesia what pad Thai is to Thailand. Possibly their best-known national dish, it's great for using up leftover rice and vegetables. Traditionally, it is served with a fried egg or omelette/omelet. Tofu can be crumbled in when frying the rice (as with the pad Thai), but I prefer to make crispy baked tofu pieces and add them with any seasonal vegetables. The roasted vegetables add taste here, but you can omit them if time is short. For this dish, firm tofu needs to be frozen and then defrosted, which changes the texture and makes it firmer and crispier when baked.

1 aubergine/eggplant, cut into bite-sized pieces
½ butternut squash, peeled, deseeded and cut into bite-sized pieces
1 tablespoon sesame oil
1 small red onion, chopped
300 g/11 oz. mixture of seasonal quick-cook vegetables, such as mushrooms, carrots, green beans, cut into bite-sized pieces
220 g/1¼ cups basmati rice, cooked (page 13), cooled and chilled in the fridge overnight
a handful of fresh coriander/cilantro leaves, sliced red chillies/chiles, and 2 sliced spring onions/scallions (optional), to garnish
lime wedges (optional), to serve

GINGER-BAKED TOFU
400 g/14 oz. firm tofu, frozen and defrosted
2 tablespoons ginger paste, or 6-cm/2¼-in. piece of root ginger, finely chopped and blended with oil
salt

STIR-FRY SAUCE
2–4 large red chillies/chiles, to taste, trimmed
4 garlic cloves, unpeeled
5-cm/2-in. piece of root root ginger, or
1 tablespoon ginger paste
3–4 teaspoons soft brown sugar, to taste
2 tablespoons soy sauce
1 tablespoon hot chilli/chili sambal (such as sriracha) or make your own Sambal (page 191)

3 baking sheets, greased

SERVES 4

Preheat the oven to 220°C (425°F) Gas 7.

For the sauce, put the chillies/chiles on a prepared baking sheet and bake for 10 minutes, then add the unpeeled garlic cloves and root ginger (not the paste, if using) and bake for a further 5–6 minutes until the garlic is golden and sticky and the chillies are starting to blacken. Put the sugar, soy sauce and sambal in a food processor or blender with the baked chillies, garlic and ginger. Process until smooth, then set aside.

Reduce the oven to 180°C (350°F) Gas 4.

Meanwhile, to make the ginger-baked tofu, squeeze out any excess water from the defrosted tofu and cut it into 2-cm/¾-in. cubes. Spread out on another baking sheet and rub with the ginger paste. Season generously with salt and bake for 15–20 minutes until golden and crispy. Set aside.

Place the aubergine/eggplant and butternut squash pieces onto the third prepared baking sheet and cook in the oven for 20–30 minutes, until softened, golden brown and crispy on the edges.

Heat the sesame oil in a wok or large pan and cook the onion until starting to soften, then add the quick-cook vegetables. Cook for 2–3 minutes, then add the sauce (for a less spicy dish, use only half the sauce). Cook for 2–3 minutes. Add the cooked rice, baked tofu pieces and baked aubergine/eggplant and butternut squash, then stir well to ensure the rice gets well coated. Stir-fry for about 2–3 minutes more until piping hot. Serve with a scattering of fresh coriander/cilantro leaves, chillies/ chiles and spring onions/scallions.

The secret to my stir-fry sauce for Mee Goreng and Nasi Goreng (page 198) is roasting the garlic and chillies/chiles before blending to create a deep, spicy sweetness. Since I don't use fish sauce, I like to find ways to create more depth of flavour in dishes that usually rely on meat or fish. You can use pre-roasted vegetables, such as the aubergine/eggplant and butternut squash from Nasi Goreng (page 198) or stick to a selection of quick-cook vegetables. The slow-baked crispy kale can be served as an accompaniment to lots of Asian dishes. It brings a crunchy element to this dish, and you can experiment with the flavouring to suit your palate, such as with chilli/chili or Chinese five-spice powder.

MEE GORENG
INDONESIAN STIR-FRIED NOODLES WITH SLOW-BAKED CRISPY KALE

100 g/3½ oz. kale
2 tablespoons vegetable oil
salt
350 g/12 oz. egg-free yellow noodles or thick, round rice noodles
a handful of cashew nuts
2 tablespoons sesame oil
1 small red onion, sliced
350 g/12 oz. mixture of seasonal quick-cook vegetables, such as mushrooms, mangetouts/snow peas, baby corn, red (bell) peppers or courgettes/zucchini, cut into bite-sized pieces
1 quantity Stir-fry Sauce (page 198)
a handful of fresh coriander/cilantro leaves, to garnish
2 spring onions/scallions, sliced, to garnish
lime wedges (optional), to serve

SERVES 4–6

Preheat the oven to 110°C (225°F) Gas ¼.

Strip the kale leaves from the stems by pinching the leaves together at the bottom and tearing them away from the thick central stem. Tear the larger pieces to about 5 cm/2 in. across.

Take two baking sheets and drizzle each with a tablespoon of vegetable oil. Scatter the kale onto the baking sheets and season generously with salt. Mix well with your hands ensuring the kale is lightly coated in the oil. Bake for 45–60 minutes until fully crisp like a wafer – you may need to remove the smaller pieces sooner, as they will crisp up more quickly. The kale turns a deeper green, like Chinese-style seaweed. Set aside to cool. The cooked kale can be stored in an airtight container for up to a week.

Put the noodles in a large bowl and fill three-quarters full with boiling water and a quarter full with cold water. Soak for 20 minutes, then drain in a colander and set aside.

Toast the cashew nuts in a dry pan over medium heat for 1–2 minutes, stirring occasionally, until golden, then chop and set aside.

Heat the sesame oil in a wok or large pan, add the onion and cook until starting to soften. Add the vegetables and cook for 2–3 minutes, then add 80 per cent of the sauce mixture. Cook for 2 minutes.

Add the soaked noodles and the remaining sauce mixture, then stir well, ensuring everything is well coated. Stir-fry for 2–3 minutes.

Place a heap of the vegetable noodles on a large plate, then scatter with fresh coriander/ cilantro leaves and spring onions/ scallions. Add a handful of crispy kale, then scatter some chopped cashews over the top.

Serve with wedges of lime.

GORENG PISANG
DEEP-FRIED BANANA

Tempura-style batter is a naturally vegan batter. It is not supposed to contain egg, which tends to make it heavier and less crispy. I had a memorable experience of eating deep-fried bananas when we were sailing down the Nusa Tengarra – a string of islands from Bali through to Lombok, Sumbawa, Rinca, Komodo (home of the infamous dragon) and finally Flores.

There were fourteen of us aboard a basic Indonesian-style fishing boat, with a raised platform for sleeping and a dug-out canoe that serves as a lifeboat. What the crew lacked in safety awareness they made up for with their cooking skills. After a full day of snorkelling and trekking about the islands, they would conjure up huge platefuls of food from their little burner at the back of the boat, nasi and mee goreng, tahu campur and deep-fried fruit. One day I woke up before everyone else, so I clambered to the front of the boat to watch the dawn break. As the sun broke across the horizon, and with dolphins leaping alongside us, one of the crew handed me a deep-fried banana, which he had drizzled in some syrup. It was possibly the most all-round spectacular breakfast I've ever enjoyed.

vegetable oil, for deep-frying
150 g/1 cup plus 2 tablespoons plain/all-purpose flour
1 tablespoon baking powder
a 750-ml/25-fl oz. bottle of ice-cold fizzy water
1 teaspoon caster/superfine sugar
1 teaspoon vanilla extract
2–3 ice cubes
100 g/1 cup cornflour/cornstarch
4 bananas, peeled and cut lengthways
4 tablespoons maple syrup or golden/light corn syrup

SERVES 4

Heat a wok or large pan of vegetable oil for deep-frying over medium–high heat to 190°C (375°F).

Sift the flour and baking powder into a large bowl. Stir in 500 ml/2 cups of the water, then add more if needed to make a medium batter not as thick as porridge. Gently whisk in the sugar and vanilla into the bowl, then add the ice cubes. Put the cornflour/cornstarch in a separate bowl.

Test the oil is ready by adding a little batter mix, to ensure that it sizzles. Working quickly, dip the bananas in the cornflour/cornstarch and then into the batter to coat all over. Lay them gently in the hot oil and fry for 2–3 minutes on each side, in batches, until deep golden brown and crispy, turning once or twice. Drain on paper towels. Drizzle with maple syrup, and serve immediately.

INDEX

PICTURE CREDITS

All travel photography by Lee James apart from:

Key: a = above; b = below; r = right; l = left; c = centre

16 l Damien Simonis/Getty Images; 16 cl Peter Adams/Getty Images; 16 br Marina Ramos Urbano/Getty Images; 17 l Maciej Dakowicz/Alamy; 17 c John Elk III/Getty Images; 17 r Gurjeet Singh Chaggar/Getty Images; 30 l Don Bolton/Getty Images; 30 c Maremagnum/Getty Images; 38 c Grant Dixon/Getty Images; 38 r Anand Purohit/Getty Images; 60 c Grant Faint/Getty Images; 126 cl Peter Ptschelinzew/Getty Images; 126 ar Ania Blazejewska/Getty Images; 126 br www.sergiodiaz.net/Getty Images; 127 l LatitudeStock – Stuart Pearce/Getty Images; 127 c Matthew Micah Wright/Getty Images; 150 l Yasmine Awwad/Getty Images; 150 cl Kevin Clogstoun/Getty Images; 150 ar Paul Kennedy/Getty Images; 151 Matthew Micah Wright/Getty Images

Acknowledgements

First and foremost, my best friend and husband Lee, who was brave enough to believe in my crazy ideas and hit the road with our young family, and whose love, support and belief in me has been life changing. I'm also indebted to my children, Tevo and Roisin, for forgiving my summer absences and sharing my love of food and travel.

I'm hugely grateful for the team behind the book. To Clare Winfield and Emily Kydd who have astounded me with their passion and skill, and in making my food look so beautiful. Tony Hutchinson, who went the extra mile on several occasions. Megan Smith and Kate Eddison, who have designed and edited my work into something more than the sum of its parts. Cindy Richards, Julia Charles, Leslie Harrington, Mai-Ling Collyer and everyone involved at RPS, and my agent Clare Hulton. You have all made this process such a fantastic experience for me. Please can we do it all again?

My journey into food has led me to many new friendships and collaborations. Claire Kelsey, Andrew Critchett, Cathy McConaghy, Lee Pointon, Christian Lambert and Richard Johnson for demystifying the world of street food, and helping me keep going when I thought I couldn't. Michael Harrison, David Fox and Mark Lloyd for their wise words of experience and support. And Debbie Halls-Evans, my steadfast cheerleader and talented friend, who makes our time in the kitchen together feel nothing like work.

This list would be far from complete without acknowledging my MasterChef family, both old and new. Karen Ross, David Ambler, Vicki Howarth, Rachel Palin, Lucy Hards, Antonia Lloyd, Ange Morris, Frances Adams and all the team at Shine. Gregg Wallace and John Torode, who made me believe I was good enough to cook for a living. Tim Anderson, Sara Danesin and Tom Whitaker, who helped me raise my game and brought me unexpected and valuable friendships.

I'm immeasurably thankful to Natalie Bismire, my travel buddy and demon slayer, who makes me believe there's nothing I can't do. Matthew and Donna Wilson for giving me a home from home when London calls, and so much more. And to Kate and Ami, whose adventures continue to inspire me everyday.

There are many acknowledgments to be made, for so many reasons beyond this list. You all know why you're listed and thank you. Natalie Coleman, Guy Wallwork, Kay Greenwell, Jessica Francis, Hannah Quirk, Joanne Smith, Hilary Cooke, Daniel Manicolo, Lisa and Sean O'Farrell, Richard and Jo McGawley, Jenny Large, Paul Adams, Tony Short, Ceri Short, Zamira Pereira, Nicola Reynolds, Francesca Raphael, Clare Major, Mark Ellis, Stuart Reeve, Sabrina Ghayour, Elizabeth Allen, Jamie Munro, Ian Munro, Yotam Ottolenghi and Michael Caines.